THE SPIRIT OF A SOUND MIND

THE SPIRIT
OF A SOUND MIND

by

JOHN R. COBB

ZONDERVAN PUBLISHING HOUSE
GRAND RAPIDS, MICHIGAN

For God hath not given us the spirit of fear;
but of power, and of love, and of a sound mind.
— II Timothy 1:7

ACKNOWLEDGMENTS

FIRST WORDS OF APPRECIATION must go to my wife, Ruby M. Cobb, who has contributed greatly by her kindly and constructive criticism as the manuscript took form and for her tireless effort in typing the manuscript.

Quotations from *Leaves of Gold*, an anthology of prayers, memorable phrases, inspirational verse and prose, from the best authors of the world, both ancient and modern, are used by permission of the publishers, The Coslett Publishing Company, Williamsport, Pennsylvania.

The quotations marked Phillips are reprinted with permission of The Macmillan Co. from *The New Testament in Modern English*, by J. B. Phillips. Copyright © J. B. Phillips 1958.

Also, quotations from *The Minister's Manual*, 1961, compiled and edited by Rev. M. K. W. Heicher, Ph.D., are used by permission of the publisher, Harper and Brothers, New York.

Others have contributed with encouragement to write this volume. Without their help and encouragement, I could never have spoken my dream aloud.

JOHN R. COBB

INTRODUCTION

MEN AND WOMEN EVERYWHERE are experiencing tensions, frustrations, emotional maladjustments, and difficulties in personal relationships. All men must confront the inevitability of the stresses of life. For all are under the sentence of life. From birth until death there will be many questions as to why this or why that, to which man cannot give an answer. The minister may console by saying, "The Lord gives and the Lord takes away." The psychiatrist may teach acceptance — but he cannot justify God's ways to man.

Most of man's troubles begin with his rebellion against God. Then follows unconscious conflict within himself. The conflict may be both spiritual and psychic — illnesses involving the depths of personality which Paul Tillich calls its "ultimate concerns." The grace of God can free man from the basic cause of these conflicts and make possible the cure of the soul. The Apostle Paul said, "I do not consider myself to have arrived spiritually, nor do I consider myself already perfect. But I keep going on, grasping ever more firmly that purpose for which Christ grasped me. My brothers, I do not consider myself to have fully grasped it even now, but I do concentrate on this: I leave the past behind and with hands outstretched to whatever lies ahead, I go straight for the goal." All who want the spirit of a sound mind should set themselves this sort of ambition. If at present one does not understand this, yet he may find that this is the kind of positive attitude which God is leading man to adopt.

In this effort to offer help to the troubled soul, we may confuse the roles of psychotherapy and religion. Bishop Sheen has described theology as "in a certain sense, a psychology, since its primary interest is the soul." It seems that in order to make the ministry relevant to man's problems, it is quite proper for the clergyman to practice a logotherapy. There are many crises of personality that are not traceable to unconscious processes. Since man is always deciding what he will become, the realization of his latent capacities is at least as important as the probing of his past. Depth psychology must be complemented by a "height" psychology that relates the future to the present. Psychoanalysis has helped man to understand backward, but religion helps men to live forward.

In the chapters of this book the writer seeks to help the reader by stimulating his capacity for responsibility and to help him become aware of the full spectrum of possibilities for personal meaning and values of life.

CONTENTS

THE SPIRIT OF A SOUND MIND

I   THE SPIRIT OF A SOUND MIND

> *For God hath not given us the spirit of fear;*
> *but of power, and of love, and of a sound mind.*
> — II Timothy 1:7

THE CHILDREN OF EVE are constantly being undone by the whispered promises of the evil one — "ye shall be as God." This is a subtle, devilish lie, skillfully calculated to destroy man. What would man give to be like God? The answer is — his soul.

Man recklessly drives God from his life and almost hysterically insists on absolute autonomy. Any hint or suggestion that his position is a dependent one, or that his dream is the delirium of a pride-infested will, is met with redoubled effort to prove his own self-sufficiency. For modern man this prideful insistence is likely to take the form of a fanatic struggle to get to the top, to get ahead.

The insistence upon unqualified freedom of soul results inexorably in the alienated man. He has staked everything upon his choice and lost everything — even the "spirit of a sound mind." He has become an alien from the commonwealth of Israel, and stranger from the covenant of promise, having no hope, and without God in the world. The devil has blinded his mind lest the light of the glorious Gospel of Christ, who is the image of God, should shine unto him.

Man refused to believe and Satan seized the power to blind his thoughts. The power to see aright and to choose wisely was gone.

> Men spurned His grace; their lips blasphemed
> The Love who made himself their slave;
> They grieved that blessed Comforter,
> And turned against Him what He gave.
>
> — *Faber*

Erich Fromm suggests that the alienation so prevalent in contemporary life is a form of idolatry. It represents the elevation of man's relative autonomy to an absolute position. Self-idolatry will lead to self-contempt. Man will not like what he sees in himself for long. Both are theologically and psychologically linked together in the processes by which man loses the spirit of a sound mind. One's mind may be likened to a garden which may be intelligently cultivated or allowed to run wild; but whether cultivated or neglected, it must and will bring forth. If no useful seeds are put into it, then an abundance of useless weed-seeds will fall therein, and will continue to produce after their kind. The Biblical view of self-idolatry where the idol represents one's own life force in alienated form is the wasted substance of the prodigal son, the buried treasure of the anxious one-talent man.

The storm gathers; man has now entered the wide gate and the broad way that leads to destruction, and many fellow-travelers pass along it. The way widens as men walk in it. Restraints upon natural appetites are thrown off. Beware of the first temptation to sin.

From thence read on the story of his life,
His proud carriage, his faulty ways,
His conquer'd foes, his fights, his toil, his strife,
His pains, his poverty, his sharp assays,
Through which he spent his miserable days.

The gospel writers have recorded many of the sayings of Jesus which tell us of the tragedies of evil and the wonders of God's grace. Let us look at two examples:

And they arrived at the country of the Gadarenes, which is over against Galilee. And when he went forth to land, there met him out of the city a certain man, which had devils long time, and ware no clothes, neither abode in any house, but in the tombs.

When he saw Jesus, he cried out, and fell down before him, and with a loud voice said, What have I to do with thee, Jesus, thou Son of God most high? I beseech thee, torment me not. (For he had commanded the unclean spirit to come out of the man. For oftentimes it had caught him: and he was kept bound with chains and in fetters; and he brake the bands, and was driven of the devil into the wilderness.)

And Jesus asked him, saying, "What is thy name?" And he said, Legion: because many devils were entered into him. And they besought him that he would not command them to go out into the deep.

And there was there an herd of many swine feeding on the mountain: and they besought him that he would suffer them to enter into them. And he suffered them.

Then went the devils out of the man, and entered into the swine: and the herd ran violently down a steep place into the lake, and were choked.

When they that fed them saw what was done, they fled, and went and told it in the city and in the country. Then they went out to see what was done; and came to Jesus, and found the man, out of whom the devils were departed, sitting at the feet of Jesus, clothed, and in his right mind: and they were afraid. They also which saw it told them by what means he that was possessed of the devils was healed.

— *Luke* 8:26-36

The demoniac was more like a wild beast than a human being. The Gerasene madman was the terror of the neighborhood. Attempts had been made to fetter him, but with the strength of frenzy he had always burst his bonds, and he roamed over the mountains, howling and bruising his naked body against the sharp rocks.

The modern psychiatrist may contend that the Gerasene madman was mentally ill. This case is almost to ridiculous to require disproof. What kind of disease was it that cried out, "What have I to do with thee, Jesus, thou Son of the most High God?" Since when has a monstrous physical distemper appeared which begs permission to enter into a great herd of swine and destroys them in a few fleeting moments? Whether one believes the man was demon possessed or mentally ill, he will agree that his mind was not sound.

Before we leave the Gadarene, let us note the great transformation which took place. The devils were cast out of the man. When the crowds came to see what Jesus had done, they found the man out of whom the devils were departed, sitting at the feet of Jesus, clothed and in his right mind.

What had happened? Jesus, the wise physician had healed the man. There was no doubt about it. Had they not seen it with their own eyes? His frenzy was calmed, and he had yielded to the will of Jesus.

Let us look at the second example:

A certain man had two sons: And the younger of them said to his father, Father, give me the portion of goods that falleth to me. And he divided unto them his living.

And not many days after the younger son gathered all together and took his journey into a far country, and there wasted his substance with riotous living. And when he had spent all, there arose a mighty famine in that land; and he began to be in want. And he went and joined himself to a citizen of that country; and he sent him into his fields to feed swine. And he would fain have filled his belly with the husks that the swine did eat; and no man gave unto him.

And when he came to himself, he said, How many hired servants of my father's have bread enough and to spare, and I perish with hunger! I will arise and go to my father, and will say unto him, Father, I have sinned against heaven, and be-

fore thee, and am no more worthy to be called thy
son: make me as one of thy hired servants.

And he arose, and came to his father. But when
he was yet a great way off, his father saw him, and
had compassion, and ran, and fell on his neck, and
kissed him. And the son said unto him, Father, I
have sinned against heaven, and in thy sight, and
am no more worthy to be called thy son. But the
father said to his servants, Bring forth the best
robe, and put it on him; and put a ring on his hand,
and shoes on his feet: and bring hither the fatted
calf, and kill it; and let us eat, and be merry: For
this my son was dead, and is alive again; he was
lost, and is found. And they began to be merry.

— Luke 15:11-24

This parable makes an amazing declaration. A sinner is
not merely a lost possession, he is a lost child of God; and
the Father's heart yearns for his recovery.

Things had not gone well with this boy. He had squan-
dered his inheritance in prodigality. Had things gone well
with him, he would have felt never a qualm, but when he
came to himself, it was not his sin but his misery that
troubled him. The god of this world blinds the minds of
those who believe not, lest the light of the glorious Gospel
of Christ, who is the image of God, should shine unto them.

When the prodigal son came to himself, he claimed himself in terms of here and now. The swine's bean-pods and
his wretchedness were inescapable reminders of his wasted
inheritance, and were a part of the reality which brought
him to his senses. In truth he did not repent at all until

he was in his father's embrace, and then his heart melted. Is not this the lesson that Jesus here teaches, that it matters not what brings a sinner to God? It is enough that he should perceive his need and lift up his eyes to heaven and cry, "Who shall deliver me from the body of this death?" The answer is, "I thank my God, through Jesus Christ, our Lord."

The returning of the lost son was an occasion for great joy. Before he could make his petition for a hireling's place, his father was shouting to the slaves: "Bring forth a robe, the best in the house, and put it on him, and give him a ring for his hand and shoes for his feet; bring the fatted calf, slay it, and let us eat and make merry, forasmuch as this my son was dead and is alive again, was lost and is found." Oh, the wonder of God's love!

> O love, that wilt not let me go,
> I rest my weary soul in thee;
> I give thee back the life I owe,
> That in thine ocean depths its flow
> May richer, fuller be.
> *— George Matheson*

The patient, Thomas, was referred to the clinical psychologist in a prison by a social worker who characterized the patient as "probably the most hopeless individual I have ever seen." Thomas' personal history certainly bore out his contention. He began correctional institutionalization at the age of ten for truancy. At twenty-five, when first seen by the clinical psychologist in a prison, he had already accumulated thirteen years of correctional experience.

Thomas accepted the invitation for therapy. He agreed to talk with the therapist one hour at a time for ten consecutive weeks, during which time the therapist shared with Thomas his personal faith in Christ. Follow the tenth session, the therapist had an eleventh session with Thomas to discuss what he had achieved. They came to a full and complete agreement that the therapy seemed to be an evident failure.

About four months later the therapist received a request from Thomas to interview him and sent for him immediately. Thomas came to the point at once. He said, "The funniest thing happened to me Saturday. I don't know if I am crazy or what. Nothing like this ever happened before. I was walking across the yard, going over to a group of people I knew, and as I was walking I suddenly experienced something. It came over me like a cloud. I couldn't move. Suddenly I felt peaceful and happy. I felt clean, pure, good, and wonderful. I don't know how long it lasted, maybe a second, maybe a minute. I have only a memory of it, but I do know that this feeling had something to do with you."

Thomas' conversion experience was much like that of Saul's on the Damascus road. His problems were not all solved, but God had now given him the spirit of power, and of love, and of a sound mind.

One aspect of man's sin is a deep fear, a feeling of uncleanness, and a sense of guilt. Adam and Eve tried to hide from God after they had sinned. They were ashamed of their nakedness. Sin had affected their relationship with God and with each other. They tried to cover themselves with fig leaves, thinking this would drive away the sense of shame and fear. The experience of the first man and woman is typical of all sinners.

The greatest problem for both God and man is sin. Man's redemption has cost God a great deal; yes, even more than the creation of the world cost Him. For freedom from sin and slavery is made sure for man in the sacrifice of Jesus Christ, God's only Son. This comes to man as a free gift. The thirty-second Psalm gives one of the finest descriptions of the blessings of forgiveness. The "forgavest" of verse five is a perfect indication that forgiveness is immediate, at the moment of confession. The Apostle John said, "If we confess our sins, he is faithful and just to forgive us our sins, and to cleanse us from all unrighteousness." Paul the Apostle, describing our status before God, said, "There is therefore now no condemnation to them which are in Christ Jesus." There is no verdict of guilt for the Christian.

One may ask, "Is forgiveness or justification just legal fiction?" No, it is true. The Word of God says so, and the new life surging in our hearts, the feeling of cleanness, the sense of wholeness, and the witness of the Holy Spirit are satisfying assurances of the new life within.

The glory of a conversion experience may be described in these lines — "God who said, light shall shine out of darkness, has shone within my heart." Yes, something has happened comparable to the great *fiat lux* of creation's dawn. It is the birth of light and order, of purpose and beauty, the ending of chaos and night. It is like the time when the morning stars sang together, and all the sons of God shouted for joy — for God hath not given us the spirit of fear, but of power, and of love, and of a sound mind.

Paul Tillich observes that the root of the word "salvation" means being healed and whole. "Saving a person," he maintains, "is healing him." The analogy makes of such "healing" a powerful religious symbol, one often used in the Bible.

The tendency to claim for religion a secular payoff merits no encouragement. Slogans such as "The family that prays together stays together," may imply a religious solution to problems that are not truly religious and they appeal to motivations far from spiritual. Dr. Abraham Kaplan said, "A faith sustained only by expectation of rewards — a mental or physical cure in the individual or in society — indicate a real sickness of soul."

The Rev. George C. Anderson, head of the National Academy of Religion and Mental Health, points out that many regular church goers like to think of religion as a tranquilizer, when, in truth, it is a way of life. To be sure, the times are troubled and we need all the help we can get. But our religion is not vital when we turn to it only for what we can get out of it. Bishop James Pike recently declared, "When religion is sold as medicine, it is being sold short." Religion can serve a therapeutic end. So can music. But it is not as medicine that these can enrich life.

Religion is not childish, as Freud claimed, but immaturity may express itself childishly in religion as in any other thing. Paul said, "When I was a child, I spoke as a child, I understood as a child, I thought as a child, but when I became a man, I put away childish things." Childishness is often displayed in our prayers. We ask for things more than we offer praise and adoration. Prayer is never petition only. It is also expressions of gratitude and humility that stem from a mature awareness of one's limitations and dependence upon God.

Once man realizes his limitations and his dependence upon

God, then he is in a position to trust Him for all those things which contribute to the spirit of a sound mind.

PRAYER

Father, we thank Thee for the spirit of power
and of love, and of a sound mind.
Help us to be aware of our limitations
and of our dependence upon Thee.
We pray in the name of Jesus Christ, our Lord.
Amen.

II   THE FOES OF A SOUND MIND

*He that dwelleth in the secret place of the most
High shall abide under the shadow of the Al-
mighty. I will say of the Lord, He is my refuge
and my fortress: my God; in him will I trust. Surely he shall deliver thee from the snare of the fowler,
and from the noisome pestilence. He shall cover
thee with his feathers and under his wings shalt
thou trust: his truth shall be thy shield and buckler.
Thou shalt not be afraid for the terror by night;
nor for the arrow that flieth by day; nor for the
pestilence that walketh in darkness; nor for the
destruction that wasteth at noonday.*

— Psalm 91:1-6

WHAT AN APPALLING catalog of foes! They are not peculiar to any one life; they haunt the precincts of all lives.
They pervade all changing hours and varied moods of the
day.

In one or the other of these changing seasons we may
all be found. There is an enemy about us in the night time,
in the daytime, in the noonday, and other foes inhabit the
twilight of evening and dawn.

There are many things which become terrifying in the

27

night time. The faint sounds of night become laden with alarming significance. The banging of the screen door by the wind, or the scratch of a tree limb on the window pane, or the howling of a dog outside, is suggestive of the unfriendly approach of an enemy.

As it is with the hearing, so it is with the sight. In the night time we become victims of exaggeration. The opaque shadows are filled out into portentous completeness. A boulder or small tree represents itself as a crouching foe. The molehill becomes a mountain. This is equally true of life in the Spirit. The real is substituted for the imaginary. We see through distorted lenses. Everything rears itself into calamitous proportions. Small obstacles or small objects become enlarged and multiplied. Recall a few lines from Edgar Allen Poe's writings: "I look upon the scenes before me — upon the mere house and the simple landscape features of the domain, upon the bleak walls, upon a few rank sedges, and upon a few white trunks of decayed trees— with an utter depression of soul which I can compare to no earthly sensation more properly than to the after-dream of the reveler in opium, the hideous dropping of the veil. There was an iciness, a sinking, a sickening of the heart, an unredeemed dreariness of thought which no gooding of the imagination could torture into aught of the sublime— and see that things are not what they seem." It is altogether possible for one to lose the clearness and calmness of his mind.

Imaginary fears can produce hell in one's mind as we see in the following story: When the patient entered psychotherapy, she was overwhelmed with fear about the disintegration of mind which she was experiencing and which was observable in her facial tremors, trembling body and cowering demeanor. Upon her was the pallor of death, and her face and eyes were those of a person making a last futile, wild struggle for life. Her body seemed frail and limp with defeat. Instead of going to his chair, the therapist touched her head in a gesture of sympathy, whereupon she put her head against him and clung to him, releasing the sobs that had not been able to come. When she spoke, it was of her fear and of this final defeat — terrible defeat after the long, uphill struggle. "Oh, Doctor — I'm so scared," she cried. This is part of the enemy's forces which the Psalmist speaks of as the "terror by night."

A man's enemies may be begotten of sunbeams as well as of darkness — "the arrow that flieth by day." The rays of light may become the arrows of death. How often it happens when men come into the clear happy light of favor, some better part of their being is slain. Bill had been a hard-working man all his life. The people of the community thought well of him. In his late thirties he acquired a large tract of rich land. Soon a change began to take place in him. He lost interest in others who were also struggling to get ahead — to get on top in the business world. He began to think in terms of self-grandeur.

He had been spared the terror by night, but had been pierced by "the arrow that flieth by day," and holy sympathy was destroyed. An arrow had slain his geniality, his spirit of good fellowship, and the winsome thing lay dead.

Note the emphasis of the dangers of the brightening day— "the destruction that wasteth at noonday." It marks the perils of the cloudless noon. This is the time when a man's life has passed into the full blaze of a fierce prosperity. Ambition has reached its greatest heights.

Kim was only thirty-eight years old but he had reached the top in the business world. He had a lovely wife, two children, a home, a nice bank account and two cars. But his reverence for God was destroyed. Pride had supplanted the grace of lowliness, and cocksureness had jostled out the spirit of a quiet walk with God. "The destruction that wasteth at noonday" had felled a giant. "Pride, like a magnet, constantly points to the object — self; but like the magnet, it has no attractive pole, but at all points repels," says Colton. In "Paradise Lost" Milton portrays Satan's fall as a consequence of his prideful resistance to gratitude. The prince of hell explains it thus:

> "I disdained subjection, and thought one step higher
> Would set me highest, and in that moment quit
> The debt immense of endless gratitude,
> So burdensome, still paying, still to owe."

There is a singular and striking illustration of this in the biography of George Frederick Watts, the eminent artist. The author calls it one of the saddest stories in the annals of art. A mature man came with his paintings and drawings to Dante Gabriel Rossetti and begged the great poet-painter to give him a candid opinion of them as to whether they were worthless or not. Rossetti looked at them carefully, wondering how he could break to the poor man the fact that there was nothing good in them whatever, and eventually he gave the man to understand this as kindly as he could. The man then drew out from under his coat another collection of drawings, and spreading them out, said that they were the work of a young student. Rossetti was delighted, exclaiming that the young student would distinguish himself. "Ah, sir," said the man, "I am that student." Somewhere between youth and manhood, the destruction that wasteth at noonday had broken in upon him, and the glory and the dream had disappeared from life.

When the brightness of the afternoon begins to grow dim in the shadows of the on-coming night and a chill air touches the happy and comfortable spirit, there is great danger of one's life becoming possessed by "the pestilence that walketh in darkness." As winter strips the leaves from the trees around us, so that we may see the distant regions they formerly concealed, so old age takes away our enjoyment only to enlarge the prospect of the coming eternity.

Most of us are familiar with the ills that plague man when life comes into the shadows. There is the pestilence of fretfulness and melancholy, of murmuring and despair. "Despair," said Charron, "is like a froward child, who, when one of this toys is taken away, throws the rest into the fire for madness. He grows angry with himself and revenges his misfortune upon his own head."

Loomis* remarks that most of us would be afraid to take the needed steps to know ourselves. We refuse to plumb our depths because we fear that in looking for something good we shall also find something horrible. We fear the emergence of an aspect of ourselves that will be unaccept-

* *The Self in Pilgrimage*, Earl A. Loomis. Harper and Row.

able to society. We even fear that the very search itself will be condemned, assuming that in questing for the self we should be so selfishly preoccupied as to be insensitive to the needs of others. We know all too well that in both the religious and the social world such preoccupation is not approved.

These fears, as I have already shown, are largely overestimated. They are within us, in our minds. Psychoanalysis has laid bare the concrete facts of what has been intuitively known all along — that there is no real foundation for most of our fears. These pseudo-hells can be transcended or escaped by seeing them for what they are.

> Grow old along with me!
> The best is yet to be —
> The last of life for which
> the first was made.
> — *Browning*

Perhaps no one knows, or ever will know, exactly how and when tensions, frustrations, emotional maladjustments, and difficulties in personal relationships begin. It is fruitless to ask where all these things come from as a prerequisite to their proximate elimination. Let not the foes of the child of God cause him to despair. There are charts and pilots to guide and guard him on his pilgrimage.

> Jesus, Saviour, pilot me
> Over life's tempestuous sea:
> Unknown waves before me roll,
> Hiding rocks and treacherous shoal;

Chart and compass come from Thee,
Jesus, Saviour, pilot me.
                              — Edward Hopper

For centuries man has viewed himself through the lenses supplied by this philosopher or that healer. Why not turn to God as the Creator and Sustainer of the universe and of the life of each man? He alone knows the basic truth of man's nature.

O Lord, thou hast searched me, and known me.
Thou knowest my downsitting and mine uprising,
    thou understandest my thought afar off.
Thou compassest my path and my lying down,
    and art acquainted with all my ways.
For there is not a word in my tongue, but, lo,
    O Lord, thou knowest it altogether.
Thou hast beset me behind and before,
    and laid thine hand upon me.
                              — Psalm 139:1-5

The key to the spirit of a sound mind is the discovery of and the surrender to Him who holds all life in His hands. This discovery and surrender is not left up to chance; God has taken the initiative "in Christ, reconciling the world unto himself."

Now let us turn away from our foes and contemplate some of our resources. The poet suggests at least two: "He shall cover thee with his feathers." This is a poetic symbol of God's protection. If God be for us, who can be against us? His wings will enfold us so that there is no possible opening for the dangerous foe to approach. Perhaps Jesus was thinking about this symbol of divine over-shadowing when He said, "How often would I have gathered thy children together even as a hen gathereth her chickens under her wings, and ye would not." There is healing under His wings. Again Jesus said, "Let not your heart be troubled," and "Come unto me, and I will give you rest."

Pseudo-health is no better when it is gained through religion. There are many who listen to voices that promise health and happiness, peace and pleasure, success and adjustment as the reward for right thinking and doing. A self-confrontation with God may not solve all of life's problems, but a real experience of God's grace will result in a spirit of a sound mind. This is basic for the wholeness of man, for man's life depends on what fills his mind. A good (whole) man gives out good from the goodness stored in his heart; a bad (sick) man gives out evil from his store of evil.

The poet was not satisfied with the figure of the mother bird in the previous verse, so he adds another: "His truth shall be thy shield and buckler." His truthfulness or trustworthiness shall be our shield and our buckler. The shield may appear to be only a partial defense, but the buckler is an all-surrounding coat of mail, covering the believer on every side. God's revealed Word is the sword of the Spirit. It is both our defensive and our offensive weapon. Trust God and be the victor over the foes of a sound mind.

PRAYER

Father, we thank Thee for making
all these provisions for us.

We pray not for ourselves only,
    we pray for our enemies also.
Help us to turn unto Thee with all
    the counsels of our hearts.
May we see more clearly, and trust
    Thee more surely.
In the name of Jesus. Amen.

III   LIVING ONE DAY AT A TIME

Therefore I say unto you, Take no thought for your life, what ye shall eat, or what ye shall drink; nor yet for your body, what ye shall put on. Is not the life more than meat, and the body than raiment? Behold the fowls of the air: for they sow not, neither do they reap, nor gather into barns; yet your heavenly Father feedeth them. Are ye not much better than they? Which of you by taking thought can add one cubit unto his stature? And why take ye thought for raiment? Consider the lilies of the field, how they grow; they toil not, neither do they spin: And yet I say unto you, That even Solomon in all his glory was not arrayed like one of these. Wherefore, if God so clothe the grass of the field, which to day is, and to morrow is cast into the oven, shall he not much more clothe you, O ye of little faith? Therefore take no thought, saying, What shall we eat? or, What shall we drink? or, Wherewithal shall we be clothed? (For after all these things do the Gentiles seek:) for your heavenly Father knoweth that ye have need of all these things. But seek ye first the kingdom of God, and his righteousness; and all these things shall be added unto you. Take therefore no thought for the morrow: for

the morrow shall take thought for the things of itself.
Sufficient unto the day is the evil thereof.

—Matthew 6:25-34

AMERICANS ARE SPENDING over one million dollars annually for tranquilizers, sometimes known as "mood" or "happiness" pills. Although doctors differ about their value, even about their safety, these little packages of synthetic bliss are being consumed at an ever-increasing rate by people fleeing from anxiety and nervous tension.

Why are these pills in such demand? Why are so many people in such a jet-propelled swivet? Is it the pace of modern living? This is a phrase dear to our hearts. Jesus offered this suggestion — "Take no thought for your life." Cease to be anxious about things of this life, for anxiety about these things is a mark of one's attempting the impossible. Dr. Phillips translates this verse thus: "Don't worry about living — wondering what you are going to eat or drink, or what you are going to wear." The old English word "thought" meant anxiety or worry, as Shakespeare said, "The native hue of resolution, is sicklied o'er with the pale cast of thought."

"Take no thought" is a command not to have the habit of petulant worry about food and clothing. The command can mean that we must stop such worry if already indulging in it. The evil of such worry is that a man's mind is divided. The potential powers which God has given him are made inoperative. The ghosts of tomorrow stalk in with all their hobgoblins of doubt and distrust. Jesus repeats the prohibition in verse 31. He did not mean to encourage a reckless neglect of the future, for the notion of proper care and forethought appears in many places in the New Testament. Fear is an uncomfortable emotion, to say the least, and too much of it can be disastrous.

It is an error to think that, since too much fear is bad, all anxiety is to be avoided. There is a good reason for our capacity to feel fear — that of self-preservation. Some anxiety is good for one. A few years ago the late Edward R. Murrow, interviewing the young English actress, Claire Bloom, on "Person to Person," asked a question to which he obviously expected an affirmative answer. "Claire," he said, "does the rush and hustle of New York ever make you long for the more placid peace of London?" The actress replied, "No, I like it, it does me good; I think I need it. I think everybody needs it."

Miss Bloom was saying that we need the steady anxiety that keeps us doing our best from day to day and makes us rise to an emergency when one comes along. This is echoing a truth which is coming to be widely recognized many years after William James, one of America's great teachers and psychologists, enunciated it. This truth was re-expressed in recent years by Dr. Ralph W. Gerard, professor of neurophysiology at the University of Michigan. A little anxiety, he points out, is good for one. It brings into use brain cells otherwise inactive, it heightens attention, improves performance, releases certain hormones, and facilitates learning by a greater spread of nerve messages in the brain.

In a recent interview, ex-president Eisenhower said, "Today we talk atomic bombs instead of muzzle-loading rifles. But we've got to learn how to live with this. Some tension, as long as we haven't eliminated the cause, is a good thing because it means alertness. We learn to live with it and still not destroy our lives."

The test of this truth is that it works. This is the doctrine of the man of action. A man may not know what he can do or will do until he is faced with a situation which calls for straight thinking and physical strength.

The following story demonstrates how fear can help us. A truck driver was pinned in the cab of his wrecked truck. While other people stood around wondering what they could do, a big Negro man walked over to the truck and pulled off the door. Then with his bare hands he put out the fire around the victim. After tearing out the steering wheel, he crawled in beside the man and pushed up the top of the truck so the victim could be pulled out. Then the rescuer disappeared. When discovered several days later, reporters asked him to explain how he had done what seemed so impossible. He replied, "A man don't know what he can do until another man is hurting." A certain amount of tension is an unavoidable part of living, and a certain amount of anxiety is a sign of life.

The word "life" in the gospels occurs in three senses: the life principle in the body, the seat of the thoughts and emotions on a par with the heart, the mind, and the spirit, and as something higher that makes up the real self. Life may be compared to a sunbeam. One day a scientist unintentionally caught a sunbeam. As the light danced on the glass in his hand, he turned the prism, saw the golden gleam give up its rainbow colors, and wondered. He did not understand what he saw. He only knew that sunlight was red, blue and green — not just white. Human life is a lot like a sunbeam; its many colors may be seen in the varied experiences of men. Life may be lost or saved. It should be the chief object of a man's care.

Jesus says three things regarding anxiety about worldly matters. *First,* it is unreasonable. Learn a lesson from the providence of God. Jesus said, "Look at the birds in the sky; they never sow nor reap nor store away in barns, and yet your heavenly Father feeds them. Are you not much more valuable to him than they? Consider how the wild flowers grow. They neither work nor weave, but I tell you that even Solomon in all his glory was never arrayed like one of these! Now if God so clothes the flowers of the field, which are alive today and burned in the stove tomorrow, is he not much more likely to clothe you, you 'little-faiths'?" Learn to live one day at a time.

Second, anxiety about worldly matters is useless. Which of you, though ever so anxious, Jesus asks, can add a single cubit to the length of his life? Fretting about the future avails nothing. To be worried about tomorrow shows a lack of common sense, for each day brings its own burden of anxiety. "One day's trouble," says Phillips, "is enough for one day." A rancher whose home stood in the line of a flash flood, saw all his possessions swept away in an hour. He was almost in despair until his little daughter reminded him, "Daddy, you still have us." Then he began to be thankful to God for His mercies, even in this time. Returning to the ranch, he wandered out to the creek. Here all the topsoil had been washed away, and in the rock there was a glittering streak. There was gold on his ranch! So all our deepest troubles may have blessings hidden in them, if we trust God to reveal them to us.

The story above is not offered as a typical day of trouble. There are crises which develop out of common day-by-day experiences. There are tensions caused by sickness, stemming from differences of opinion, approaching parenthood, social competition, and increased responsibility, etc.

Third, anxiety about worldly matters is irreligious. Jesus said, "After all these things the heathen seek." The gospel of the pagan world is obviously this: lay up for yourself all you can get here and now. Ask any heathen — a man's prime job is to provide his family with the best and to lay up something for his golden years. He must provide well. The world says he deserves the finest, best, biggest, and newest of everything. Be solicitous for tomorrow. Consider the pension in the field and how it grows!

The Apostle Paul had been buffeted by the messengers of Satan. Three times he had begged the Lord for relief. The Lord's reply was, "My grace is enough for you." Our Father does not give grace today for tomorrow's needs; He gives sufficient grace for this day's trouble. He will do the same for tomorrow.

It is an error in judgment to ignore the fact that anxiety is usually caused by something specific, and to believe that swallowing a pill will make that something go away. The problem will still be there in the morning and so will the temptation to ignore it or to reach for another pill. Learn to face troubles with God's enabling grace. Recall Moses' blessing on the tribe of Asher — "As thy day, so shall thy strength be." Isaiah's word to Israel was, "They that wait upon the Lord shall renew their strength, they shall mount up with wings as eagles; they shall run and not be weary;

they shall walk and not faint." He is a fortunate man, and a happy one, who lives one day at a time.

Too many people are existing on the growing edge of life. They are spectators instead of participants in the race of life. They need a divine stirring up of their natural propensities as Moses beautifully relates God's dealings with Israel in Deuteronomy 32:11 (RSV):

> Like an eagle that stirs up its nest,
>   that flutters over its young,
> Spreading out its wings, catching them,
>   bearing them on its pinions.

To really live is to be aware of a vitality that has in it great promise. There is the prospect of new lands to conquer, new frontiers to cross with limitless horizons which beckon and call. Life can be an exciting adventure.

The happiest people in the world today are those who give of themselves to others. Jesus strongly recommended it with these words: "Freely ye have received, freely give." People have different things to give. Some have time, energy, skills, and ideas. Others have some special talent. All of us can give appreciation, interest, and encouragement — which require no money expenditure unless for a postage stamp or a telephone call. Mr. J. C. Penney, founder and director of J. C. Penney Co., says that the philosophy of giving yourself away actually works. This is not surprising, because Jesus taught it many years ago. Adelaide Love expresses the same idea in the following verse:

> In giving, we learn most blessedly,
> That He, to whom we give, gave more than we,

He may have needed our poor gift, indeed,
But, oh, to give it was our greater need.
— *Adelaide Love,* in *War Cry*

The basic presupposition of Jesus' life in both teaching and living, in helping and healing, in success and in apparent defeat, is that God, His Father, could be trusted completely. His teaching everywhere punctuates this basic attitude and understanding. Knowledge of this fact is a means of liberating mankind from the destructive power of fear. The birth of faith in Jesus Christ points the way toward the goal of the rehabilitation of the whole man.

"Faith," says Paul Tillich, "is a total and centered act of the personal self, the act of unconditional, infinite and ultimate concern." This concern is about oneself and the infinite to which he belongs. The question now arises: What is the source of faith? It is the gift of God. If, then, it is the gift of God, how may one receive it? The secret of faith is very near. It is the burden of our preaching. Faith, you see, can only come from the hearing of the message of Christ.

Jesus gave a great many signs in the presence of His disciples to prove that He was the Christ, the Son of God, with power to heal and to forgive. Look at one example: Jesus was on His way to heal Jairus' daughter who was dying. It was of the utmost importance that He should arrive on time. But as He went, the crowds nearly suffocated Him. Among them was a woman who had had a hemorrhage for twelve years and who had derived no benefit from treatment. "She had suffered many things," says Mark, "of many physicians, and had spent all that she had, and had re-

ceived no benefit, but rather had grown worse." This is not
surprising when one considers the methods of the physicians of that period.

Pliny mentions their prescription for the ailment in question, specifying among the rest, a poultice of fresh ass's
dung and a draught of goat's urine. It is little wonder that
unflattering things were said about physicians in those days.
"To live under doctor's orders," said one Latin proverb, "is
sorry living." "A doctor," said another, "is worse than a
robber. The robber takes your money or your life; the
doctor takes both." It is written in the Talmud that "the
best of doctors is ripe for Gehenna." We can be thankful
that modern medicine has come a long way from such
methods.

The woman came up behind Jesus and stealthily touched
the edge of His cloak. She thought, *If I can only touch his
clothes, I shall be healed.* She was certain that Jesus could
heal the sick. She may have thought that there was magi-
cal efficacy in merely touching Jesus. One may think that
it was a superstitious idea, but there was faith in it, and
her faith was richly rewarded. Straightway the fountain
of her blood was dried up, and she perceived in her body
that she had been healed of the plague. The woman pur-
posed to steal away unnoticed, rejoicing over her cure, but
a greater blessing was in store for her. Jesus had felt the
touch of trembling faith and promptly responded to the
mute appeal. It had unlocked the flood-gates of His pity
and His power.

Jesus stopped and turned around in the midst of the
crowd and said, "Who was that who touched my clothes?"

He must have known that the woman would confess of herself. When everyone denied it, Peter remonstrated, "Master, the crowds are all around you and are pressing you on all sides." "Somebody touched me," replied Jesus, "for I felt that power went out from me." The woman, trembling, came forward and fell at His feet, telling the whole story. "Daughter," said Jesus, "it is your faith that has healed you — go in peace." Had Jesus suffered her to steal away, she would have lost the healing of her soul. She would have remained a stranger to His love.

This was not an unusual or a hard thing for Jesus to do. Isaiah said to Ahaz, "Ask thee a sign of the Lord thy God; ask it either in the depth, or in the height above, is there anything too hard or too difficult for Him?" No! These boundless resources are available to all who turn to Him in faith. For both tomorrow and today are in the hand of God whose power is great enough to complete our incompleteness, and whose mercy and forgiveness are adequate for the evils which we introduce into both the present and the future.

PRAYER

Father, we thank Thee for Thy
    wonderful promises.
May we rest with complete assurance
    in Thy love and care.
Forgive our faltering faith and strengthen
    us for the work of Thy kingdom.
In the name of Jesus we pray. Amen.

IV   PUTTING ENERGY INTO DOING SOMETHING WORTHWHILE

> *I have fought a good fight, I have finished
> my course, I have kept the faith: Henceforth
> there is laid up for me a crown of righteousness,
> which the Lord, the righteous judge, shall give
> me at that day: and not to me only, but unto
> all them also that love his appearing.*
>
> —II Timothy 4:7-8

BERNARD SHAW ONCE WROTE, "To have leisure is to bother about whether you are happy or not. The cure for it is occupation, because occupation means preoccupation and the preoccupied person is alert, active and alive — which is pleasanter than happiness." In a recent newspaper article Dr. Crain remarked that 33,000 people, who need no medical care, go weekly to physicians for treatment. Dr. Crain's prescription for these people is, "Go to work, or better still, join some church and become engaged in creative activities. Learn to give yourself freely in some work for others as well as for yourself."

From the beginning, the development and well-being of man's distinctive faculties, intellect, emotions, and will power, were related to his use and control of the possessions in the world around him. He was to "keep it" (the world) as God had created it and intended it. His work became more difficult because of his sin. He became subject to such hardships in making a living as were not contemplated at first.

Hard work is a cure for uncontrolled anxiety. This was demonstrated in the life of the Apostle Paul. He was a man of action; he became the chief exponent of the Christian movement. The story of his life and work is found in the book of Acts and in the thirteen epistles he wrote.

"The glorious fight that God gave me," said Paul, "I have fought." This was a favorite figure with him. The "fight" is the contest of his struggle for Christ. It is impossible to put too much emphasis on the life and work of Paul. His life shows a good pattern for us. Look at a summary of his sufferings:

I have worked more than any of them.

I have served more prison sentences!

I have been beaten times without number.

I have faced death again and again.

I have been beaten the regulation thirty-nine stripes by the Jews five times.

I have been stoned once.

I have been shipwrecked three times.

I have been twenty-four hours in open sea.

In my travels I have been in constant danger from rivers and floods, from bandits, from my own countrymen, from pagans. I have faced danger in city streets, danger in the desert, danger on the high seas, danger among false Christians. I have known exhaustion, pain, long vigils, hunger and thirst, doing without meals, cold from lack of clothing.

Apart from all external trials, I have the daily burden of responsibility for all the churches.

How did Paul do it? What was his secret? The words of Shakespeare may be enlightening:

> Sweet are the uses of adversity
> Which, like the toad, ugly and venemous,
> Wears yet a precious jewel in his head.

Learning to face trouble calls for progressive exposure to inconveniences and minor difficulties. Patience is a virtue here. Let it be remembered that steadfast application to a fixed aim is the law of a well-spent life. "Every noble work," said Carlyle, "is at first impossible." "All growth," remarked Calvin Coolidge, "depends upon activity. There is no development, physically or intellectually, without effort, and effort means work. Work is not a curse; it is the prerogative of intelligence, the only means to manhood, and the measure of civilization." Life will be fruitful in ratio to how it is lived out in noble action or in patient perseverance. Endurance is the measure of a man.

The Apostle Paul had learned how to live when things were difficult and when things were prosperous. He knew the secret of facing the evils of either poverty or plenty. The source of strength for all things was through the One who lived in him — Jesus Christ.

> Like a star
> That shines afar,
> Without haste
> And without rest,

Let each man wheel with steady sway
Round the task that rules the day
And do his best.

— *Goethe*

A few years ago Samuel Goldwyn phoned his life-long friend, Cecil de Mille, asking him to have lunch with him the next week.

"I would love to, Sam," Cecil said, "but you see, I'm flying over to Rome in a couple of days to open The Ten Commandments there. Then I fly to France and Germany and hop around Europe for other openings. And after London, I jump back to Hollywood to start supervising a picture, and then . . . ."

"Cecil," said Goldwyn to this 76-year-old youngster, "you have the right idea. The harder you work the longer you'll live."

Cecil chuckled, "Tell that to the American people. I know it — I wonder if they do."

There is nothing more stimulating than being busy, and there is nothing more disheartening than vainly trying to find something worthwhile to absorb all of one's attention and effort. The happiest and best adjusted people are those who are busy doing much-needed work. One's mind may be likened to a garden which may be intelligently cultivated or allowed to run wild; but whether cultivated or neglected, it must and will bring forth. If no useful seeds are put into it, then an abundance of useless weed-seeds will fall therein, and will continue to produce after their kind. Herbert Hoover, among many others, agrees with this thought. On his eighty-second birthday he warned that one must not retire completely from working — "or you will shrivel up into a nuisance to all mankind." Mark well the words of Charles Kingsley: "Thank God every morning when you get up that you have something to do that day which must be done whether you like it or not. Being forced to work and forced to do your best will breed in you temperance and self-control, diligence and strength of will, cheerfulness and contentment, and a hundred virtues which the idle never know." George Bernard Shaw says that "the true joy of life is in being used for a purpose recognized by yourself as a mighty one."

Too many people have lost the interest or will to work. They are looking for some great inspiration. The gospel of work is never popular to some, for man is so constituted that he is always looking for an easy way. Don't wait for inspiration — put your energy to work. It was Edison who said that genius is one per cent inspiration and ninety-nine per cent perspiration.

Balzac, the writer, spoke of himself as "plying the pick like an entombed miner, for dear life." His work was toil, not the supposed easy flow of inspiration. Flaubert speaks of himself as "sick, irritated, the prey, a thousand times a day, of cruel pain, but continuing my labor like a true working man, who, with sleeves turned up, in the sweat of his brow, beats away at his anvil, whether in rain, or blow, hail or thunder."

One day the great composer, Haydn, was asked why he had never written a quintet; his answer was: "Because I was never commissioned to write a quintet." Stevenson, the poet, knew that he was not long for this life, and he used to say, "Even if you know you will never complete your folio, get started on your next page." This is the spirit of a sound mind.

There came a time when Paul could say, "I have finished my course." He had used this metaphor of himself to the elders at Ephesus. Then the course was ahead of him. Now it is behind him. He could now say, "Lord, thou deliveredst unto me five talents: behold, I have gained beside them five talents more." There is a little sadness in the thought — "I have finished my course" — but not for long, for there is much joy in the finishing of a good work.

A few years ago Ramon Navarro, the movie star, said, "As I look back on my life and my career, I consider it worthwhile because the money I earned went to help others. I hope the cast of MGM's current version of 'Ben Hur' will be able to know the same contentment when they reach sixty. I, therefore, pass on to Charlton Heston and all the others the words of a Durango dentist: 'Always save some portion of your money for old age,' and 'money is worthless unless it helps people.'"

There were thirteen children in Navarro's family, and out of his subsequent earnings he brought every one of them, including his parents, to California. He supported the whole family. Some of the dividends of his investment may be listed: one brother is an architect, another is a dentist, a third is a sound engineer, and a fourth is a geologist. Two of his sisters are nuns, one in Mexico City, one in Madrid, and the others are happily married.

Faith plays an important part in a man's life and work. The word "faith" has two main senses — fidelity and belief. As Paul looked back over his life, he believed that he had been faithful to Christ. He had not deserted. Faithfulness to God in performing the work of Christ was the key-note of his character. The world needs this type of faithfulness today, not only in matters of religion, but in world affairs as well, Justice Warren Douglas said, "These days I see graft and corruption reach high into government. I see people afraid to speak their minds because someone will think they are unorthodox and therefore disloyal. We need the faith that dedicates us to something bigger than ourselves and our possessions, for this is the most critical period of world history."

Paul looked into the future with satisfaction as he said, "The future for me holds the crown of righteousness." He did not mean that faith is sustained only by expectation of rewards. He had received mercy himself and knew not how to hold his peace. He saw souls perishing; he felt confident in the power of his Master's message to meet the need of every man's soul. To this end he invested his life. Now the time for a higher recognition was drawing near. There are three kinds of crowns for the Christian — the crown of righteousness, the crown of life, and the crown of glory. Each one is a reward for achievement.

Jesus declared that sacrifices for the kingdom would be repaid. "We have left everything and followed you," said Peter, "what is that going to be worth to us?" To claim for religion a secular payoff merits no encouragement, but it is quite clear in the reply that Jesus gave that there would be a reward, not only in the next world, but a most generous one in this world. "Every man," said Jesus, "who has left houses or brothers or sisters or fathers or mothers or children or land for my sake will receive it all back many times over, and will inherit eternal life."

Every man performs his work in expectation of the fruits which it will bring forth. The justification for the laboring is in the harvest. There is satisfaction in performing one's appointed function without reference to the outcome of the work. Faithfulness brings joy, peace, and contentment of mind. All these gifts are too precious to buy. The following illustrations are suggestive of this truth.

A woman of means whose life had shriveled into a plaintive mass of egocentric despair, remarked, "I hate myself!" Her hatred for herself was the payoff for a life dedicated to caring for no one but herself.

Then there was little "Debbie" of the comic strip who said to her playmates, "I feel wonderful today. I was just thinking how nice it is just to be me." Her feeling of well-being was the result of her relationship with, and her care for others.

Man's very nature makes it impossible for him to reach completion and fulfillment in history. Looking beyond this world to the world to come and the receiving of the rewards which the Lord, the righteous judge, shall give at that day, is the crown of faith — the meaning of human existence.

Put energy into doing something worthwhile. Make God's interest your supreme concern. His concern is as wide as life itself. Leave all lesser interests in His hands. Here is the secret of a quiet heart. "Nothing," says St. Chrysostom, "makes men light-hearted like deliverance from care and anxiety, especially when they may be delivered therefrom without suffering any disadvantage, forasmuch as God is with them and stands them in lieu of all." Keep in mind the law of spiritual action and reaction. He who works sparingly shall reap also sparingly; he who works generously shall receive a generous reward. Put yourself to work at some good task that will absorb all your attention and energy. For action and work use up the energy which fear creates in us. This will help one to keep or maintain the spirit of a sound mind.

PRAYER

Father, we thank Thee for the good works
    which Thou hath ordained.
Forgive us wherein we have failed
    to walk in them.
Help us that whatever we do today
    will bring glory to Thy name. Amen.

V   THE MEDICINE OF A MERRY HEART

A merry heart doeth good like a medicine.
— Proverbs 17:22

THREE QUARTERS OF A CENTURY AGO, before the organization man and his colleague in the gray flannel suit made their appearance, Robert Louis Stevenson wrote, "Look at one of your industrious fellows. He sows hurry and reaps indigestion; he puts a vast deal of activity out to interest, and receives a large measure of nervous derangement in return." Today's industrious fellows are no better off. The heat is on for more of them and nervous derangements are far more common.

"My wife seems more interested in meeting the right people than in finding happiness for ourselves," a businessman complained to the Rev. Hugh Hostetler, a counselor at the American Foundation of Religion and Psychiatry in New York. The man had just become a branch manager for a large concern; for the first time in his life he felt that he could relax and enjoy life. "Instead," he said, "with my wife's social ambitions, I feel I'm at the bottom of the hill all over again."

There came to the great physician, Dr. Arbuthnot, a very dejected and miserable patient. When Dr. Arbuthnot examined him, he found nothing physically wrong with the man. "Why, all you need is cheering; go and hear that delightful clown, Grimaldi." "Alas! Doctor," the patient replied, "I am Grimaldi."

No prescription is half so medicinal for certain states of the body as the possession of a merry heart. Every doctor knows that a merry heart relieves nervous tensions.

"No one knows exactly why we laugh, or why anything that is funny should cause us to make such a peculiar noise. It would be just as logical to stick our thumbs in our ears and wiggle our fingers as it is to giggle, bellow or howl with laughter. But when something strikes our funny bone, our diaphragm flutters up and down, and we are moved to give out laughter.

"The urge to laugh appears early in life. Babies smile, then coo, and finally chuckle when pleased. If certain parts of the body are tickled with the fingers, laughter is produced in babies as well as in many adults. But by the time a child starts to school, he also laughs at things he hears and sees. He does not need to have his ribs tickled in order to giggle." *

Laughter is a sane and health response to the innocent foibles of men, and to some which are not innocent. A good example of the humorous situation is found in some of the unbelievable questions tourists have asked their patient guides. One shock-proof viewer gave the mighty Grand Canyon a fast look and asked, "Where's the golf course?" "Isn't any," replied the ranger. "What are you supposed to do around here," demanded the tourist, "look at the scenery?"

The classic observation about Carlsbad Caverns came from a tourist moved to comment: "Well, sir, it sure looks like the farther down we go, the deeper it gets."

A visitor in Yellowstone, staring at the steaming, spouting geyser asked, "Do you keep Old Faithful running in the winter?"

On a high pass in Great Smoky Mountains National Park a chilly visitor said in surprise to a ranger naturalist, "Say, does it ever get this cold up here?"

Perhaps the reason for laughter in these cases is that every one feels that he is better off than the victim, and feels superior to him.

If a man meets a lady on the street, tips his hat to her and his toupee falls off, revealing a bald head, most of the people who see it will roar with laughter. Or if a person gives someone else a "hotfoot" and the victim leaps into the air, howling with pain, everyone laughs at his pain except the one whose foot hurts. This is called the humor of the unexpected happening.

Laughter is our recreation to immediate incongruities and those that do not affect us essentially. For instance, if a proper and well-dressed man sits in a chair and the chair fails to hold him up — spilling him upon the floor — we laugh. We laugh at the proud man falling on the floor, not merely because the contrast between his dignity and his undignified plight strikes us as funny, but also because we feel that his discomfiture is a poetically just rebuke to his dignity.

Here is another example. A woman telephoned postal authorities in Dallas and complained about the substitute mail carrier on her route. "The regular carrier gets along with our dog," she explained angrily, "but every time the substitute makes the route it upsets the dog."

"Where is the dog now?" asked the postal authority.

"Oh, he's under our mimosa tree."

"And where is the mail carrier?"

"He's up in the tree. It's upsetting my dog and making him bark."

Everyone laughs at the man up the tree. He does not belong there, and the situation is incongruous.

Human existence itself is filled with incongruities. Man is a creature who shares all the weaknesses of the other creatures of the world. Life does not always make sense. Things happen to us. The best of our plans fail because of one evil or another. To meet the disappointments and frustrations of life, the irrationalities and contingencies of life, with laughter, is a high form of wisdom. It does not obscure or deny the dark irrationality of our incongruities. It merely yields to them without too much emotion and friction. Laughter is good like a medicine.

"Situation humor need not be described in words. However, a great part of humor is told rather than seen. Certain words are funny in their very sounds, such as 'bobble' and 'squirt.' Sometimes people get mixed up in pronouncing their words, and instead of saying 'people think' they might say 'thinkle peep.'" * People usually laugh at such mistakes.

The Freudian Fumble, a simple slip of the tongue, causing one to say what he had been thinking secretly but did not want to express, is always good for a laugh. An example is the story of a minister who was conducting a program on a Detroit TV station. He was reading excerpts from viewer's letters of encouragement, taking care to display the donations clipped to each one. Then looking straight into the camera he said, "And now, my dear funds . . . ."

Another instance is the story of a young mother who was expecting a visit from her minister — who had a very big nose. She had warned Johnny, her son, not to say anything about it. Then, at tea, she leaned over and asked the minister, "Reverend, how many lumps of sugar will you have with your nose?"

Laughter may express a mood which takes neither self or life seriously. The idiotic fool turns life into a comedy. Everything is one big joke. In this case laughter has ceased to be good medicine and has become the instrument of irresponsibility.

"Humor of words may take many forms. It can be gentle and kindly, or it can be harsh and biting. There is no exact line of distinction between these various types." * But most people agree on general definitions.

"*Satire* presents the weaknesses of mankind and makes fun of them." * Usually the satirist attempts to cure man's foibles and weaknesses by making people laugh at them. There were those who thought that we could laugh Mussolini and Hitler out of court. Now some think we can laugh the Russian leaders out of court. But laughter alone has never destroyed a great seat of power and authority in history.

Irony is a tricky sort of humor. It may begin as a compli-

* Reproduced from *The World Book Encyclopedia* with permission. Copyright © 1956 by Field Enterprises Educational Corporation. International Copyright © 1956. All rights reserved.

ment or a simple statement. But there is a concealed sting in the remark which the hearer may not feel at first. For instance, a catty hostess said to a guest, "How lovely you look, dear — you must have gone to a lot of trouble."

Sarcasm is another sort of humor which is much more brutal than irony or satire. Its essential quality is bitterness or taunting reproachfulness. It may or may not be ironical, but always it is cutting or ill-natured. Sarcastic laughter is better against real evil, partly because it senses its impotence to deal with it seriously. Such bitter laughter of derision has its use as an instrument of judgment.

What is true of our condemnation of each other is true of the condemnation of God against us. In the Holy Bible God is pictured as laughing at man and having him in derision:

> He that sitteth in the heavens shall laugh:
> the Lord shall have them in derision.
> — *Psalm* 2:4

There is no suggestion of a provisional geniality in God's laughter. The people have imagined a vain thing. The kings of the earth set themselves, and the rulers take counsel together against the Lord and against His anointed. Therefore, divine laughter of derision is pure judgment.

In the words of our text, "A merry heart doeth good like a medicine," the proverb maker was not thinking of the effect upon oneself, but rather of the effect upon others. But here again the law of spiritual action and reaction works. Do good like a medicine to others, the reaction will be good for the doer as well.

The roots of genuine merriment, medicine for oneself and others, is in self-forgetfulness. "If you want to be miserable," said Charles Kingsley, "think about yourself, about what you want, what you like, what respect people ought to pay you and what people think of you." No one should think just of his own affairs, but each one should develop a deep interest in the welfare of others. Happiness is a perfume you cannot pour on others without getting a few drops on yourself. The words of Thomas Hughes are very applicable here, "Blessed are they who have the gift of making friends, for it is one of God's best gifts. It involves many things, but above all, the power of going out of oneself, and appreciating whatever is noble and loving in another." Never act from selfish motives or personal vanity, but in humility, think more of others than you do of yourself.

The merry heart is more self-forgetful; it is also a trusting heart. One can laugh at the incongruities of life when he remembers that his Helper is omnipotent, gracious, full of compassion, slow to anger, and of great mercy. It is told of Mr. Spurgeon, the great preacher, that while driving home in his carriage one day, he suddenly, and without assignable cause, burst out into hilarious laughter. It had suddenly struck him how absurd it was to worry as he had been worrying that morning, when he had a splendid word like this to lean upon: "My grace is sufficient for thee." Today and tomorrow are in the hands of God. His grace is equal to all our needs. His promises never fail.

Jesus again and again made merriment a dominant note in the kingdom music. He came eating and drinking. The world has never fully understood the gladsome mood of Jesus. His good news may expose one to the fires of shame confessed to God and man, but the fires are refining fires and their suffering is not worthy to be compared with the deep joy bestowed. The kingdom music sweeps through all the cadences of unrestrained tides of delight.

There is a river whose waters rise with the tides of the sea. Miles inland muddy banks are filled, grounded boats are floated. Occasionally the inrush takes the form of a wave. The people on that river call the wave "the Aegir." The boys cry on its approach, "The Aegir, the Aegir!" It is a name of noble origin in Icelandic myths, the name of the Giant of the Calm Sea, and it has remained in the language of the people of that river as the signal of the early Norse invaders. Tennyson who lived in the same western country, caught the picture of that calm sea:

> But such a tide as moving seems asleep,
> > Too full for sound and foam,
> When that which drew from out the boundless deep,
> > Turns again home.

The joy of the Christian is like an Aegir. It floods every inlet. It floats all the vessels of delight in our souls. It is good like a medicine in the heart and life of all mankind.

PRAYER

> Father, we thank Thee for the joy that
> > may be ours in Christ Jesus.
> Make us to hear joy and gladness;
> > uphold us with Thy free spirit.
> Help us to be a channel of Thy joy
> > to all our fellows.   Amen.

VI THE RECOVERY OF FAITH IN GOD

> *Why art thou cast down, O my soul? and*
> *why art thou disquieted in me? hope thou in*
> *God: for I shall yet praise him for the help of*
> *his countenance.*
>
> —Psalm 42:5

THE POET KNEW that something was wrong in his life. It no longer tasted good; he was cast down and depressed. The words, "cast down," describe a feeling of anxiety, guilt, and despair which had crept into his heart. He wanted to know why he was cast down and depressed in his soul. Then he realized that he had lost faith in God. "Hope thou in God" was the answer to his need.

To be aware of one's loss of faith is a healthy sign. Sin blinds or darkens the mind. It is the work of the Holy Spirit to convict one of his lack or need. In the recovery of faith in God, one must start again at the beginning. Remove the cause. Then build on a solid foundation.

> The steps of faith fall on the seeming void,
> But find the rock beneath.
>
> — *Whittier*

All men live by some kind or some portion of faith, be it articulate or inarticulate. Some may live by false faith for a time; men can meanly exist on the basis of a meager or impoverished faith. If one's "little faith" is not nourished and does not grow strong, one becomes vulnerable to evil. Moses, in Genesis, describes sin as waiting like a wild beast for its prey. When a man has gone his own way, thinking that he is able to face his own problems in his own strength, he is dangerously near that state in which he can no longer keep evil out of his heart. The words of Browning are so true:

> Just when we're safest, there's a sunset-touch
> A fancy from a flower-bell, some one's death,
> A chorus-ending from Euripides —
> And that's enough for fifty hopes and fears
> As old and new at once as nature's self
> To rap and knock and enter in our soul.

No one who is experiencing doubt is safe from this beast of prey. This is one of the supreme facts of life which one should never forget.

Faith may be compared to a beautiful diamond, its many facets sending forth light and strength into all areas of life. Tillich defines faith as a total and centered act of the personal self, the act of unconditional, infinite and ultimate concern. Ultimate concern means this: "You shall love the Lord your God with all your heart and with all your soul, and with all your might." This is unconditional surrender to God. It is a centered act of trust of the whole self to God.

The question now arises: What is the source of this all-embracing and all-transcending faith? You will recall what was said in an earlier chapter — faith is the gift of God. Like all good and perfect gifts, faith comes from God's great treasure and is made available in Jesus Christ, His Son. Yes, all the boundless resources of God are available to all who turn to Him in faith.

Another question arises: How can I receive such faith? The secret is very near you. Faith, you see, can only come by hearing the message, and the message is the word of Christ. The faith that comes by hearing is not merely a passive receptivity, but a positive embrace of the good news that is heard, which involves the hearer's participation as well as his sense of sound. What is heard by the heart springs into action on the lips as a confession and flows directly into a life of thankful obedience. This makes hearing an urgent business. The human heart is the soil in which the good news of Christ is planted. This message, if given a chance, will lead one to God. He is one whom you can trust completely with every detail of your life, one who cares for every sparrow in the tree, one who clothes each lily in the field; our God is a Father with an utterly dependable fatherly presence and care.

The basic presupposition of Jesus' life, in both teaching and living, in helping and healing, was that God, His Father, could be trusted completely. Faith in the wisdom and power of God's love was the inner spring of Jesus' life. His teaching everywhere emphasizes this basic attitude and understanding.

Jesus did many things in the presence of His disciples to teach them to believe in Him. I have chosen this incident so that your faith in Him may be strengthened and that you may have a fuller life as His disciple. The following is more a paraphrase than a translation and I have drawn heavily upon David Smith's *Commentary on the Gospels*.

The evening passed into night and a storm arose, but Jesus, engrossed in prayer with the Father, was all unconscious of the elemental strife. The dawn was breaking when He rose from His knees, and looking down upon the lake, He descried the boat more than half-way across, battling with wind and wave. The disciples, in sore jeopardy, were wishing that their Master were with them, when to their amazement, they saw Him near by. He was walking on the water. He made as though He would pass them by, and they did not hail Him (a little touch of sailor superstition — when a Jew met a friend by night, he would not greet him lest it should be a demon in his friend's shape). Thinking that it was a ghost that they saw, the disciples would not hail Him, but they were unable to repress a cry of alarm, and it reached Jesus. He spoke at once to them, "It's all right! It is I, myself, don't be afraid." Peter, ever ardent, ever leaping before his fellows, made reply: "Lord, if it is really You, bid me to come to You on the water." "Come on, then," replied Jesus. No sooner had he set foot on the waves than fear got the better of the impetuous disciple and he began to sink. "Lord, save me!" he cried. At once Jesus reached out His hand and caught him, saying, "You little faith! what made you doubt?" The alarm of the disciples had by this time been allayed, and they welcomed their Master aboard. The wind sank to rest and they sped lightly on their way. The whole crew came and kneeled down before Jesus, crying, "You are indeed the Son of God." To their wonder and gladness it seemed but a moment until they got to shore.

— *Matthew* 14:23-32

When Christ is absent from His people, they go on, but slowly, and with great difficulty, but when He joins Himself unto them, oh, how fast they steer their course; how soon are they at their journey's end!

Peter's performance was poor. His faith was thoroughly tested. The whole thing seemed impossible. When you are in the midst of the sea of life, tossed with the waves, and the wind is contrary, how is your performance? Is it like this disciple of little faith? His faith was small, but when he felt himself sinking he cried, "Lord, save me!" This is the cry of faith and it never goes unrewarded. The prophet Isaiah (42:3) spoke of Jesus' gentleness in these words:

> A bruised reed shall he not break,
> And the smoking flax shall he not quench.

This is an amazing story. Down through the centuries it has been a trial to faith and a jest to unbelief. According to Strauss, the peculiar difficulty of the narrative lies in the fact that the body of Jesus appears so entirely exempt from a law which governs all other human bodies without exception, namely the law of gravitation, that He not only does not sink under the water, but does not even dip into it. On the contrary, He walks erect on the waves as on firm land.

This incident has been the jest of unbelievers ever since the later half of the second century when Lucian pelted it with the pitiless artillery of his keen and biting satire. Many have since thought to explain it away. It is indeed impossible for a mortal body to walk upon the water, but Jesus was no ordinary man — He could and did control nature. The disciples could not, at the time, understand the ineffable mystery. It was enough for them to realize the wonder of their Lord and they were convinced that He was indeed the Son of God.

The words of Hezekiah, "This is a day of trouble, and of rebuke, and blasphemy," are as applicable to our own day as to his. We are living in tragic times. The great powers that have been trusted as safe custodians and protectors of the rights of all people have become vain in their imaginations, their foolish hearts have been darkened by sin. They hold a monster in their hands. This destructive power has become so great that it threatens the nations with mutual annihilation. The most obvious or immediate need of this age is an adequate faith to live by.

There are two facets of an adequate faith for our age which need mentioning. The first is a form of hope which gives meaning to life, not only by what is accomplished in history, for man's nature is such that he cannot hope to reach complete fulfillment in this life. There are times when our hopes far exceed our grasp. We need a new perspective of the meaning of the words of the Apostle Paul, "If in this life only we have hope in Christ, we are of all men most miserable." We need a faith which is both this worldly and other worldly. We must never lose heart. May these heroic words of Paul in II Corinthians 4:8-10 help us:

We are troubled on every side,
    yet not distressed;
we are perplexed, but not in despair,
Persecuted, but not forsaken,
cast down, but not destroyed;
Always bearing about in the body
    the dying of the Lord Jesus,
that the life also of Jesus might be
    made manifest in our body.

Trying things happen to us so that we may know more and more about life. Our faith is being tested, but our future is magnificent. Through the mercies of God we have been given a life full of hope. So let us brace our minds as one who knows what he is doing and rest the full weight of our hopes on the grace of God.

Queen Frederika had just returned with King Paul from an inspection tour of the little Greek island of Santorini, where an earthquake had left death and destruction. A reporter, who was visiting Athens, asked her to tell him the greatest truth she had learned from life. Her answer came promptly in lines from Walt Whitman:

From imperfection's murkiest cloud,
Darts always forth one ray of perfect light,
One flash of heaven's glory.

For one so young, Queen Frederika had lived through a number of shockingly tragic years. When she and King Paul came to the throne in the spring of 1947, Greece was in the throes of civil war. Before it ended Frederika had seen twenty thousand children made homeless and in many instances also motherless and fatherless; another twenty-eight thousand were kidnaped and whisked behind the Iron Curtain, thousands more were dead of cold and starvation.

While the war was still raging, and frequently since, she has traveled on donkey back to the rugged mountain sections of Greece where the suffering was greatest to set up children's villages and to put heart into the people. Weeping mothers have clung to her; broken, old-before-their-time fathers have wrung her hand and lonely children have rushed into her arms. Knowing these facts, one would not be surprised that she answered the reporter's question by quoting the lines from Whitman to which she added, in explanation, these simple words: "This is one of the things I have found very true in life; that it is our duty, no matter how difficult things are, to find that 'flash of heaven's glory.' It may be in the smile of children, in the expression of old women by the roadside, or any unexpected little event that gives one courage to go on."

Here, it seems to me, are true words to live by, for they show how one can find courage and hope even among all the setbacks of an imperfect world — hope thou in God.

The second facet of an adequate faith is a sense of humility which recognizes the lack of moral or spiritual strength as a common form of human weakness in which all men share. The opposite of humility is pride. Pride is at the very heart of man's sin. It compasses one about as a chain. The immediate result is a swollen estimate of one's powers or merits, then one begins to look down on others and even to treat them with insolence and contempt. Jesus exposed its danger when He catalogued it among the evils which make a man unclean, for it is from inside, from men's hearts and minds that evil thoughts arise — lust, theft, murder, adultery, greed, wickedness, deceit, sensuality, envy, slander, pride and folly. Adam blamed Eve for his sin. Eve attributed her's to the serpent. Fault finding is an old sport:

> In men whom men condemn as ill
> I find as much of goodness still,
> In men whom men pronounce divine
> I find so much of sin and blot,
> I do not dare to draw a line
> Between the two, where God has not.
> — *Joaquin Miller*

The roots of humility go down deep into an understanding of man's weakness and his dependence upon a loving God.

> God wove a web of loveliness,
> Of clouds and stars and birds,
> But made not anything at all
> So beautiful as words.
> They shine around our simple earth
> With golden shadowings,
> And every common thing they touch
> Is exquisite with wings.
> — *Anna Hempstead Branch*

Listen to God's Word — your fears will take wings and fly away. Faith, you see, can only come from hearing the message, and the message is the word of Christ.

Father, we thank Thee for the word of faith
 which Thou hast planted in our hearts.
Forgive our failure to nourish and exercise
 this precious gift.
Grant us the wisdom to feed our faith
 on the sincere milk of Thy Word,
That it may grow thereby. Amen.

VII   THE RULING PRINCIPLE OF A GOOD LIFE

He endured, as seeing him who is invisible.
— Hebrews 11:27

THIRTY-ONE-YEAR-OLD Dennis Dean Oliver, cowpuncher extraordinary, six feet three and carrying two hundred pounds on a rangy frame, stood before a capacity crowd at the Dallas Coliseum. His handsome face expressed confidence, contentment and prosperity. He was the champion calf roper of the National Finals Rodeo, the respected representative and cherished friend of fellow calf ropers. But Oliver was not always so healthy, happy, and obviously well fed.

To start with, Dean Oliver was born a "blue baby." He survived an incubator confinement, but retained a mild heart ailment. Then, after nine years of gypsy-like wandering across the country with his family, Oliver finally grew out of his childhood infirmities.

Another hindrance to his becoming a roping champion was the fact that Oliver was an Idaho boy. When Dean began cowboying in the early nineteen fifties, no northwesterner had ever won a calf-roping championship. The geographical handicap had logical root. But Dean overcame all his handicaps and in 1961, in sixty grueling rodeos throughout the country, he won $28,841.

"Dean's got speed, size, co-ordination, and he uses his head," says Bill Hinderman, one of rodeo's finest all-around champions. "But it's that little extra something he turns on when things get rough that's the secret of his success. He just plumb never gives up." This last line reveals the ruling principle of a good life.

> Every noble work is at first impossible.
> — *Carlyle*

Jesus called the twelve disciples unto Him and laid His command upon them. He sent them forth in twos to travel through Galilee, preaching and healing in His name. Before they went their various ways, He gave them words of direction and encouragement. First, He defined their mission. Then He told them how they should equip themselves. It is noticeable what pains Jesus took to disabuse His apostles of any illusions which they might be cherishing. He was calling them to strife, suffering, and sacrifice. He would have them recognize that fact and consider whether they had courage to face the ordeal and go through with it. In the midst of His address He spoke these words: "But he that endureth to the end shall be saved" (Matthew 10:22b).

These are strong words. The subject of perseverance gives rise to the question as to the certainty of the ultimate salvation of believers. Will they, without fail, endure to the end, or, are we to believe that some may fall away from their saving faith in Christ and perish? The answer to this question is — they shall never perish. One must hold on to the hope which he professes without the slightest hesitation — for Jesus is utterly dependable.

The words, "shall be saved," mean more than the forgiveness of sin. The Lord has provided salvation for all of life.

> Measure thy life by loss instead of gain;
> Not by the wine drunk, but the wine poured forth;
> For love's strength standeth in love's sacrifice;
> And whoso suffers most hath most to give.
>   — *N. E. H. King*

Jesus was unremitting in the task of preparing the twelve for the ministry for which they had been chosen. Whenever He had them alone, walking with them by the way, reclining at the table, sitting on the hillside, or sailing on the lake, He would teach them of the things that belong to His kingdom and to their vocation. There was, however, one omission which they observed and wondered at. He had not taught them to pray. One of the twelve, finding Him at prayer, appealed to Him, "Lord, teach us to pray, even as John also taught his disciples." Jesus granted the request and furnished the Apostles a model to show them what manner of petitions they should offer before the throne of grace. "Thus pray ye," said Jesus:

> Our Father that art in heaven,
> Hallowed be thy name;
> Thy kingdom come;
> Thy will be done;
> as in heaven, also upon the earth.
> Our bread for the approaching day
> give us today.
> And forgive us our debts

> as we also have forgiven our debtors;
> And lead us not into temptation,
> But rescue us from the evil one.
>
> — *Matthew 6:9-13 (Free)*

This model prayer has several striking characteristics. It is brief, simple, universal, and spiritual. There is no difficulty with the prayer itself. It concerns itself almost exclusively with the things of God and the needs of man. The difficulty arises in the need for persistence in prayer.

> And he said unto them, Which of you shall have a friend, and shall go unto him at midnight, and say unto him, Friend, lend me three loaves; for a friend of mine in his journey is come to me, and I have nothing to set before him?
>
> And he from within shall answer and say, Trouble me not: the door is now shut, and my children are with me in bed; I cannot rise and give thee.
>
> I say unto you, Though he will not rise and give him, because he is his friend, yet because of his importunity he will rise and give him as many as he needeth.
>
> — *Luke 11:5-8*

Jesus does not mean that God is like a selfish neighbor who must be plagued into compliance; neither did He teach His disciples to besiege God with importunities and insist on getting their heart's desire. The story is a warning against listlessness and half-heartedness. He is teaching that prayer is not the mumbling over of stereotyped formulae, but a serious and strenuous business demanding the undivided energy of mind and heart.

The Apostle Paul was Timothy's chief teacher of Christ. Among the many things which he taught him was "the ruling principle of a good life." The old preacher challenged the young one to endure hardship with Christ: "Thou therefore, endure hardness, as a good soldier of Jesus Christ" (II Timothy 2:3).

We are up against an unseen power that controls this dark world, and spiritual agents from the very headquarters of evil. We are not only engaged with evil, but we stand for truth and righteousness. To win the victory one must be strong and never give up. Faithful effort is a law of the good life.

Recall the quotation — "Every noble work is at first impossible." These words came from the pen of Thomas Carlyle who had learned that endurance has its rewards. Life is full of hard tasks. They are always intended to awaken strength, skill, and courage in learning how to master them.

In the words of our text, Moses is pictured as a man of great deeds. There is one thing which marks his whole course of action from the time he elected to brave the king in behalf of Israel — he endured, as seeing him who is invisible.

Moses made his great choice at a significant season of life. He made the decision neither in the heat and impulsiveness of youth, nor in the decadence of age. He made the great choice when he was grown up — when he was forty years old. This indicates that his choice was made intelligently, deliberately, and with entire decision.

The world might think that Moses made a bad decision. It involved great sacrifices. As the son of the king's daughter he had an eminent position and brilliant prospects. The reason given for Moses' refusal to be called the son of Pharaoh's daughter, his renunciation of his position in the court in order to associate himself with his oppressed fellow-countrymen was this: "he had respect unto the recompense of the reward." He knew the pleasure of sin was for a time only. There must have been plenty of evidence in and around the king's court of what sin could and would do. Had not his own people greatly suffered at the hand of the Pharaohs?

His choice exposed him to sore afflictions. It involved his identifying himself with a nation of wretched slaves who were oppressed by a grinding tyranny. It brought him into close contact and companionship with hordes of ignorant bondmen. It called him to undergo persecution as the leader of the movement for their emancipation. He made his choice at the risk of his life; for, when he had avowed it in action by killing the Egyptian slave driver, Pharaoh sought to slay him. Moses fled into the land of Midian to live.

It was forty years later in the desert of Mount Sinai that an angel appeared to him in the flames of a burning bush. He told Moses God's plan to send him back into Egypt. The years in the school of hard knocks had taught him well for the role he must now play.

So this same Moses, much wiser, whom Israel had rejected in the words, "Who appointed you a ruler and a judge?" — God sent to be both ruler and deliverer with the help of the angel who had appeared to him in the desert of Mount Sinai. This man showed wonders and signs in Egypt and was their leader in the desert for forty years — eighty years of exploits and endurance as full proof of his faith.

The real key to his endurance is in these words — "as seeing him who is invisible." Moses had learned to see the invisible One. The physical eyes cannot behold the spiritual verities of life. They have no fitness for immediate dealing with the great realities of the spiritual realm. New eyes are needed. Recall the words of Paul: "You belong to two worlds; do not miss the invisible one while you are busy with the visible one. Cultivate your vision, learn to see the realities which your eyes miss. Look through the world that is seen and discover the realities which it suggests and implies."

Cultivate your sight. It takes years for a new born child to learn to see with perspective. In the first of life, sight is confined to the ability to distinguish light from darkness — bright light causing contraction of the pupils and closure of the eyelids. By one month the eyes will follow bright objects. By the third month the infant will recognize his bottle or a similarly familiar object. By the fifth or sixth month visual impulses are stored up so that there is increasing recognition of familiar faces or objects. This learning process goes on for years. So it is in the spiritual realm. One learns to see with new eyes.

One is reminded of the word of Jesus, "Blessed are the pure in heart, for they shall see God." Goodness of heart makes for clearness of sight. The first important matter, if the astronomer would see clearly, is that he wholly eliminate the disturbance within the telescope itself. Living as we do in a world where there is much outside us to mar our spiritual vision, the first and essential thing is that we free ourselves from the disturbing currents within — pride, selfishness, and doubt, which vex and falsely bias our sight.

Before one can see with proper perspective he may need another touch of the Master's hand. Jesus asked the blind man, "Do you see anything?" He looked up and said, "I see men, but they are as trees walking." Then Jesus put His hand on his eyes once more and his sight came into focus and he recovered and saw everything sharp and clear. Yes, two treatments may be necessary. There is healing in the touch of the Master's hand.

When Holman Hunt told his artist friends that he was going to paint Christ, they pointed out the absurdity of the undertaking. "You can paint only what you can see," they said; "you will only waste your time trying to do the impossible."

"But I am going to see Him," Hunt replied. "I will work by His side in the carpenter shop. I will walk with Him over the hills of Galilee. I will go with Him among the poor, the blind, the lame and the leprous. I will go with Him to Gethsemane. I will travel with Him to Calvary and climb the cross with Him until I see Him, and then I will paint Him."

In estimating Hunt's work, Miss Bacon says: "There is no false note that shocks us, or makes us feel that, after all, the story is affected and artificial. They are sincere, truthful pictures that speak to the mind as well as to the eyes." John Ruskin declares Hunt's painting, "The Light of the World," one of the most noble works of sacred art ever produced.

It makes one feel that the great painter did live with Christ until he saw Him with his eyes.

Gerritt Beneker was once painting a man who was engaged in testing, for bridge girders, the quality of a swab of molten steel that was swung out on a crane from a blast furnace. The man stood at his work almost naked in the fierce heat, covered with sweat and grime. As Beneker, with quick strokes of his brush, caught and interpreted the skillful tester of the molten steel, another laborer who came up and was looking on as the artist painted, called to his companions in labor: "I say, fellows, come up and see this. Here is the greatest painter that ever lived. He is painting God where nobody else can see him." Some happier day perhaps others will learn to see with new eyes, and be able to catch hints and intimations of the divine presence where few suspect it now. They, like Moses, will be able to endure, "as seeing one who is invisible."

Seeing the invisible One supplied Moses with the strongest and sublimest inspiration to never give up. The realization of God's presence raised his soul above the fear of men. He was on the Lord's side; he need not fear what man could do unto him. God and man make a team which cannot be beaten. The awareness of divine presence inspires the soul with patience in the trials of life. It will enable one to see that the present distress is temporary and negligible. These little troubles, which are really so transitory, are winning for us a permanent, glorious, and solid reward out of all proportion to our pain. Seeing the invisible One is the source of energy and perseverance for the difficult duties of life. The consciousness of God's presence and approbation always imparts courage to the heart, resolution to the will, and energy to the arm of his faithful servants.

PRAYER

Father, we thank Thee for full salvation
    in Christ Jesus.
We have need of patience, that after
    we have done Thy will,
We might receive the crown of life.
    In Jesus name. Amen.

VIII LOOK UPON SUFFERING AS HEAVENLY DISCIPLINE

> *Ye have not yet resisted unto blood, striving against sin, and ye have forgotten the exhortation which speaketh unto you as unto children. My son, despise not thou the chastening of the Lord, nor faint when thou art rebuked of him: for whom the Lord loveth he chasteneth, and scourgeth every son whom he receiveth. If ye endure chastening, God dealeth with you as with sons; for what son is he whom the father chasteneth not? But if ye be without chastisement, whereof all are partakers, then are ye bastards, and not sons. Furthermore, we have had fathers of our flesh which corrected us, and we gave them reverence: shall we not much rather be in subjection unto the Father of spirits and live?*
>
> — Hebrews 12:4-9

WHEN ALBERT SCHWEITZER SAID, "The world is mysteriously full of suffering," he expressed the universally human sense of query, wonder, and mystery as to the meaning of suffering. In the presence of physical illness or handicaps one may ask, "Why must I suffer this way?" When stricken by grief, one may ask, "Why did this happen to me?"

One does not always receive satisfactory answers to his questions, but we do suggest some truths which may be helpful. It is the teaching of God's Word that much of one's suffering is the result of sin. The holy anger of God is disclosed from heaven against the godlessness and evil of men. The innocent do suffer in this life as well as the wicked. This we must learn to accept. Then, suffering may be God's plan to prove one's faith and to bring praise, honor, and glory to the sufferer.

Suffering that has meaning is bearable; in fact, it may be entered into with joy. All suffering is not physical; it may also be mental and spiritual. Adam and Eve experienced both spiritual and physical suffering as a result of their sin. At first they experienced shame and guilt. This is spiritual suffering. One must not minimize the intense or extreme degree of this kind of suffering. Read David's words, "My sin is ever before me . . . when I kept silence, my bones waxed old through my roaring all the day long . . . For day and night thy hand was heavy upon me; my moisture is turned into the drought of summer." Adam and Eve were made to bear physical suffering also. Her's included multiplication of pain and conception; his included life-long subjection to hardship in making a living — the pain or sorrow attendant upon difficulties which at first were not contemplated.

Adam's name could have been Solomon or David. The list is long — all did evil in the sight of the Lord. This brought the wrath of God upon their lives. The full penalty for sin is often delayed, as in David's case — his son also bore the consequences of his father's transgression. This is one of the tragedies of sin. Innocent children often suffer for the sins of their parents.

We are all familiar with the verses by Robert Louis Stevenson, "My Shadow," in his *Child's Garden of Verses*. It is probably among the first poems that many of us ever learned.

> I have a little shadow that goes in and out with me,
> And what can be the use of him is more than I can see.
> He is very, very like me from the heels up to the head;
> And I see him jump before me, when I jump into my bed.
> The funniest thing about him is the way he likes to grow —
> Not at all like proper children, which is always very slow;
> For he sometimes shoots up taller like an India rubber ball,
> And he sometimes gets so little that there's none of him
>   at all.

We all have a "little shadow," a physical shadow, all the time, except at night or on a dark day, or exactly at noon. But the verse fits perfectly another kind of "shadow" — our influence. Where we go, it goes, whether good or evil.

According to the theology of Jesus' day, suffering was always penal and the result of antecedent sin. This is not true. One Sabbath, when the Feast of Dedication was near at hand, Jesus, was passing along with His disciples when His eye rested on a spectacle of misery — a young man who had been born blind. The disciples assumed that sin was the cause of this man's blindness and wondered whether it had been ante-natal or hereditary. They asked Jesus, "Who did sin, this man or his parents?" Jesus rejected both alternatives. The man's blindness was no punishment at all.

It was a providential visitation, "that the works of God might be manifested in him." This was purposeful suffering.

Look upon suffering as heavenly discipline and learn how to live. This is a hard lesson for God's children to learn and to understand. One of the purposes of human suffering is for instruction in obedience. Jesus, Son though He was, had to prove the meaning of obedience through all that He suffered. In the growing up process it is important that we learn perfect obedience to our heavenly Father. Then when we have been proved the perfect sons, we become a source of comfort to all who should obey Him.

Another purpose of human suffering is "to prove your faith." Remember the words of the Apostle Peter: "This is no accident — it happened to prove your faith which is infinitely more valuable than gold, and gold as you know, even though it is ultimately perishable, must be purified by fire."

At present you may be perplexed by the suffering which you must endure and your heart may be in heaviness. But this proving can mean tremendous joy to you. Your future is magnificent. The Lord plans to bring you praise and honor and glory. "Suffering overcomes the mind's inertia, develops the thinking powers, opens up a new world, and drives the soul to action," says Anthony D. Evans.

It is courage that we need. Courage — an independent spark from heaven's bright throne, by which our souls may stand raised, triumphant, high and alone. So let us take a fresh grip on life and brace our trembling limbs. Let us not wander away from the path but forge steadily forward. On the right path the limping foot recovers strength and does not collapse. One "learns to live."

Cowards die many times before their deaths;
The valiant never taste of death but once.
— *Shakespeare*

A man was the victim of criminals and of the untamed
forces of nature. He had also fallen prey to a vile and dis-
gusting disease. His sickness was so humiliating that he re-
tired into his room — a miserable, pathetic spectacle. George
MacDonald wrote, "Must it not be a deep spiritual instinct
that drives trouble into solitude? Away from the herd flies
the wounded deer; away from the flock staggers the sickly
sheep to a solitary hiding place to die." Wayne Oates remarks that "loneliness is the aching heart of suffering. The
killing part of suffering is the way in which it cuts one off
from the land of the living." Pain makes our communion
with one another all the more difficult and all the more
poignantly necessary. In "No Exit," Jean Paul Sartre portrays three people in hell. Each one is trapped in an exitless
room. They are incapable of communicating their distress
to one another. This is hell.

The message of Christ presents just the opposite of suffering alone — the fellowship of suffering. There is a fellowship of suffering with all creation. Recall the words of the
Apostle Paul: "It is plain to anyone with eyes to see that
at the present time all created life groans in a sort of universal travail."

Then there is the fellowship of suffering with Christ in
His suffering.

He was despised and rejected by men;
a man of sorrows, and acquainted with grief;
and as one from whom men hide their faces

he was despised, and we esteemed him not.
Surely he has borne our griefs
and carried our sorrows;
yet we esteemed him stricken,
smitten by God, and afflicted.
But he was wounded for our transgressions,
he was bruised for our iniquities;
upon him was the chastisement that made us whole,
and with his stripes we are healed.

— *Isaiah* 53:3-5 (RSV)

This is redemptive suffering. The apostles had been beaten and forbidden to preach anymore in the name of Jesus. But they departed from the council, rejoicing that they were counted worthy to suffer shame for His name. Suffering that has meaning is bearable; as stated before, it may be entered into with joy. We can be full of joy here and now even in our trials and troubles.

Also, there is the fellowship of suffering with the saints of the household of God. We all live together. We are all committed to a vital spiritual fellowship. When one suffers — all suffer. A therapeutic virtue is transferred from the strong to the weak.

There is great value in suffering if taken in the right spirit. Trials and troubles will give one patient endurance; this in turn will develop a mature character, and a character of this sort produces a steady hope — a hope that will never be disappointing.

The present distress is temporary and negligible. "In my opinion," said Paul, "whatever we may have to go through now is less than nothing compared with the magnificent future God has planned for us. The whole creation is on tiptoe to see the wonderful sight of the sons of God coming into their own." We need to lay hold of God's grace. It is sufficient for us. For where there is weakness, God's power is shown more completely.

Even though one goes no further than Robert Louis Stevenson in saying, "I believe in an ultimate decency of things," such faith has inestimable value. If one can go beyond Stevenson's affirmation, the Christian religion presents the most stimulating and life-giving faith in human experience. "The maturing of a great personal life," said Fosdick, "includes handicaps, deficiencies, troubles and even moral failures."

The Christian religion is the basis for hopeful adventure and the source of available power which is sufficient for all of us. This is one thing which the saints have definitely learned. There is a beaten track down through the ages along which these wise men and women have trodden. There is great value to be gained on the beaten track.

Stephen Corey illustrates this theme: "I helped take the first missionaries to Moniecka Station in the Congo, in Africa. We were on the mission steamer, *Oregon*. A great crowd of natives gathered on the bank as we landed. Among them was their powerful chief, Lonjataka. He was not a Christian, but he gave me a greeting I have never forgotten. He stood on the bank in dignified fashion, with his long spear in hand, a girdle of leopard skin around his waist, and on his head a leopard skin cap. After the preliminary greeting, he asked me for my proverb (*losako*). I gave it to him in the native tongue: 'Love the Lord with all your heart.' Then I asked for his *losako*. His reply was, 'Tociko mbuni,' meaning literally, 'Mark the path.' The actual meaning was, 'When you pass through the dense African jungle, and come to an obscure place, or a division in the path which might confuse one, always mark it, so that the next person will find his way.' "

The "path" for a triumphant faith over suffering is marked well in the book of Job.

The book of Job is the story of a man who had tremendous spiritual courage to shake off the doubts turned loose in his heart by suffering, lack of explanation from God, and the accusations of his friends. The following lines present a poetic outburst of victorious faith over suffering:

> For I know that my Redeemer lives,
> and at last he will stand upon the earth;
> and after my skin has been thus destroyed,
> then without my flesh I shall see God,
> whom I shall see on my side,
> and my eyes shall behold, and not another.
>
> — *Job* 19:25-27 (RSV)

The accusations of Job's friends served to force the soaring faith of Job higher and higher. "Like an eagle which sets itself in the face of a storm," said Watts, "he rises completely above it." His faith is a beautiful thing.

> A thing of beauty is a joy for ever;
> Its loveliness increases; it will never
> Pass into nothingness.
>
> — *Keats*

PRAYER

Father, we thank Thee that Thou hast counted
  us worthy to suffer with Christ.
Forgive us when our hearts rebel against
  Thy heavenly discipline.
We do not pray that this cup be removed
  from us,
But give us Thy grace that we may bear
  Thy cross with joy.   Amen.

IX THE PURSUIT OF WORTHY GOALS

Not as though I had already attained, either were already perfect: but I follow after, if that I may apprehend that for which also I am apprehended of Christ Jesus. Brethren, I count not myself to have apprehended: but this one thing I do, forgetting those things which are behind, and reaching forth unto those things which are before, I press toward the mark for the prize of the high calling of God in Christ Jesus.

— Philippians 3:12-14

ONCE A NEWSPAPER ran a cartoon which showed two people looking down from Mars at the crowds of people hurrying to and fro on the earth. "Where are they going?" asked the first; and the second replied, "They are not going anywhere; they are just going." This could easily be a parable of our age. Too few people have a worthy purpose or goal in life.

Emerson said, "Hitch your wagon to a star." These six little words are a summary of man's achievements and an everlasting inspiration to the future races of mankind. From Adam to Einstein, every forward step taken by humanity through revolving centuries, every advance by mankind toward the ultimate goal, has been led by some valiant dreamer whose eyes were fixed upon the dawn of a new day.

Moses, with dying eyes, saw a star out of Jacob that blazed in the promised land. The three wise men who sought the Christ Child were led by the radiance of an eternal star to the manger in Bethlehem. Columbus pinned his faith in the dawn of a new day. Kepler announced the laws of unchanging spheres; Newton watched the apple fall from the tree; each looked beyond the present into the future.

One may have the wrong goal from the beginning. A young man wrote home from camp to his parents: "Dear Dad and Mother, we went on a trip yesterday. It was a mountain-climbing trip. It was a lot of fun except we climbed the wrong mountain."

On the other hand, there are those who undertake to reach the right goal, but confuse the whole matter by trying to reach it in the wrong way. Therefore, it is important that goals of value to the individual and to mankind be set, keeping in mind the rules in reaching the goal which will not mar the glory of the crown of achievement.

The Apostle Paul believed that a worthy purpose or goal would add meaning to life. He said, "I leave the past behind and with hands outstretched to whatever lies ahead, I go straight for the goal." If you find life empty, try putting something worthwhile into it. Set yourself some worthy goals.

Every wise man knows the value of a single victory. One may be a preacher or plumber, businessman or farmer, teacher, artist, doctor, ditch-digger — it makes no difference. Nothing succeeds like success. But we must not consider any present attainment sufficient for the present or the future. One cannot judge his capacity by past achievements. He should do much better in the future.

A seventh-grade boy came in from school. It was report card time, and this youngster had a collection of "twos" and "threes" to show for his grades. His father was not pleased. The boy responded by saying, "Well, Dad, I'm average! 'Twos' and 'threes' are average. That's what my teacher said."

Former United States Senator Goldwater says, "No one is average. We as individuals contribute to an average, but to my mind the great sin of the twentieth century is to be found in the notion so prevalent nowadays that our common goal should be to be average." We are living in a challenging world. Everyone must do his absolute best. To accept the average as being a worthy goal is to whiff the anesthetic of mediocrity. This would be a betrayal of God-given talents; each one is required to exercise those talents to the maximum of his individual ability. Excellence is the only material goal in life worth pursuing. Accomplishment to the best of one's ability brings life's only satisfactory reward.

Memory is a wonderful thing. Without it progress would be impossible.

It is memory which enables one to carry the advantages of past ages to the coming time. But memory can become a curse. This is true when one burdens memory with thoughts and feelings which cannot help, but which hinder his future development. Dante, in his *Divine Comedy,* tells us that rather than burden memory with thoughts and feelings which cannot help, but rather, hinder, one needs to drink from the river Lethe, whose waters, when drunk, cause forgetfulness of the past. The Scriptures never teach one to dote upon a golden age behind him. Hence the Apostle

Paul could say, "I leave the past behind and with hands outstretched to whatever lies ahead, I go straight for the goal."

Paul was no novice when he wrote these words. An old man, rich and ripe in many graces, far and away beyond the experience of most Christians, he still felt that he had not reached the great end of his efforts. Set some worthy goals for yourself. They will give real meaning to your life. Life is no childish game. If you find your present life empty, try putting something worthwhile into it.

A teen-ager wrote Ann Landers for advice on how to make her life a success. Mrs. Landers replied, "Make *you* your central project. Strive toward maturity." No one is born full grown. At our physical birth we do not spring like Athene, fully armed, from the head of Zeus. Dr. William C. Menninger, a distinguished American psychiatrist, has listed six important and desirable qualities present in all normal, mature, and well-adjusted people. They are (1) sincerity, (2) personal integrity, (3) humility, (4) courtesy, (5) wisdom, and (6) charity, which he defines as "the capacity to love." Dr. Menninger was speaking of mental and social maturity; but we would certainly expect the same qualities, with additional ones, to be present in a spiritually mature person. The word "perfect" in the New Testament means mature, or full grown.

The teen-ager confessed, "I don't know what maturity is." This writer suggests that maturity is many things. It means one has reached a certain age biologically — being fully developed. It means one has reached the proper height of virtue and integrity both mentally and spiritually. It is the ability to see the whole picture of life with true perspective. It means being able to choose the course of action which will pay off later. One of the characteristics of immaturity is the "I want it now" approach. Mature people are able to wait. Maturity is the ability to carry through a project or a situation until it is accomplished, finished, brought to an end. The person who is constantly changing jobs, changing friends, and changing mates, is immature.

Maturity is the ability to face the present unpleasantness, frustration, or discomfort without despair or collapse. The adult (mature) person knows that he cannot have the moon. No one wins every time.

Maturity is the ability to do what is expected of one. Recall the words of Paul: "When I was a little child, I talked and felt and thought as a child. Now that I am a man my childish speech and feeling and thought have no further significance for me." He acted in a way that was expected of a mature person.

Maturity is the ability to make a decision and then to stick with it. This requires wise thinking, forethought, and courage. It is not easy to know what is the best thing to do or to carry plans through to completion.

There are immediate goals which remain close to nature. Then there are more ultimate goals which reach the level of the spirit. The goal of the Christian should be to reach spiritual adulthood — or the measure of the fullness of Christ. There are many more worthy goals, but if one reaches the goal of spiritual adulthood, some of them will be accomplished in the same race. Rufus Jones tells us that the rewards we get from life are directly tied up with the life we have lived. "The goal," he says, "is in the process."

> I am a part of all that I have met;
> Yet all experience is an arch wherethro'
> Gleams that untravell'd world, whose margin fades
> For ever and for ever when I move.
>
> — *Tennyson*

One may never build that temple at Jerusalem, but will posterity find the plans among your papers when you pass from the scene of time? One cannot steal second base and keep his foot on first. Set for yourself a worthy goal, then go straight for it.

There are two elements in reaching a goal which one needs to keep in mind. The first is *humility*. The second is *intent*.

Humility is not cowardice. No man is craven who dares to look first on eternal splendor and then upon his own littleness. The humble are they who consent to receive the knowledge of themselves. This is a brave consent — having a deep sense of one's littleness. Nor is humility mean-spiritedness, or self-depreciation, or lack of enthusiasm.

Humility has one root in a sense of indebtedness. The food on our table, the words in our mouth, the liberties which we enjoy are, in largest measure, gifts to us from invisible helpers in the past or present.

The other root of humility is in reverence and the sense of need. When one looks up to the heavens or at the world and sees the beauty and wonder of God's work, he will confess, "Who is sufficient for such splendor?" When one sees a man inflated with pride and worshiping at the poor altar of self, some instinct tells him that this is a common form of human weakness in which all men share. In this kind of spirit we will avoid the peril of attributing our historic failures and frustrations to this or that individual.

The second element which one needs to keep in mind is intent. Intent means to fix one's mind on, direct one's attention to, the goal in order to reach it. It is a metaphor of a runner continually looking toward the goal or mark as he runs. Hence the Apostle Paul said, "With outstretched hand to whatever lies ahead, I go straight for the goal." The wise man bends every circumstance to the attainment of his goal. He even makes adverse circumstances work toward his mark. Problems may be transmuted into prowess.

From the above, one might conclude that pursuing worthy goals is like playing a game — and it is. Do you remember how, on a race track, every competitor runs, but only one wins the prize? Well, one ought to run with his mind fixed on winning the prize! Every competitor in athletic events goes into serious training. Charles Paddock endured tremendous pain to become an Olympic champion and the world's fastest sprinter — all this for a fading crown. But our contest is for an eternal crown that will never fade.

There are three words of exhortation for the one who would make the most of his life. The first is *aspire*. The second is *pray*. The third is *learn*.

Let us aspire to higher goals in the future. It is important that we go forward until we arrive at real maturity — that measure of development which is meant by "the fulness of Christ." One must not be satisfied with present attainment. Let your eye stretch forward, as over the intervening space, up to the goal.

I would ascend to lofty heights
Of snow-white purity —
Where never a flect of mire is seen,
Where never a thought, unchaste, unclean,
Can wing its flight through the smoky screen
That hides the city's shameful sights
In deep obscurity.

I would aspire to mountain peaks
Of quiet dignity —
Where never a youth from honor veers,
Where never a saint need close his ears
To ribald sounds, or despising sneers —
Where God with mortals often speaks
In sweet benignity.

I would surmount the giant steep
Of rugged honesty —
Where never a sound of guile is heard,
Where never a lie can be inferred
By subtle knaves, who would twist a word
To vex the youth who, probed he deep,
Would sight the travesty.

I would attempt the tow'ring Alps
Of Christ-like lowliness —
Where never a soul strives first for fame;
Where never a king may state his claim,

Unless he bear a blameless name
That, by its majesty, he helps
The cause of holiness.
> — *A. R. Wiggins* in *War Cry*

Each man can set a higher goal. It will keep him from being careless. He needs to bend his energies toward that which is difficult of attainment, toward that which will require singleness of heart and intensity of soul. This will give greater meaning to life.

Any one of us can fall into error, so let us pray against this danger. One can be earnest in the main, and yet there may be some particular thing in which there is self-satisfaction, about which one is not sufficiently enlightened, and so he will wander from the right course. Pray and "even this will God reveal unto you."

Lancelot the knight was one of the mightiest of men, a man of magnificent strength, yet he failed in the quest for the Holy Grail, and did not flinch to confess the cause of his failure:

> . . . but in me lived a sin
> So strange, of such a kind, that all of pure,
> Noble and knightly in me twined and clung
> Round that one sin, until the wholesome flower
> And poisonous grew together, each as each —
> Not to be plucked asunder.
> > — *Tennyson*, "The Holy Grail"

Lancelot failed because the worries of this life and the illusions of wealth choked his good intentions to death. No failure need be final. One may always look to God to show the way when in error.

Let us learn from past experiences. Paul said, "Only whereunto we have already attained, by that same rule let us walk." One must not recall past victories for self-contentment, but for lessons to be learned. If one has attained any skill in the Christian life, it is because he has followed Christ and His teachings as his rule — by that same rule let us walk.

One not only runs the race with determination, but he also "runs that he may obtain." There are rules of the contest which one must obey or be disqualified. These rules are discussed in another chapter of this book. However, there are two basic rules which need to be stated here. One is faith in Jesus as Saviour, and the other is faithful effort in running the race of life.

The above may seem to be elementary teaching, but there is much food for thought here. What one does with his life will be determined by these two basic laws. To fail to live by them is to fail in life. To live by them is to succeed in life.

What was the secret of Paul's strength? It was not in his health, for he suffered from some bodily illness. It was not in his earthly wealth, for he had given up all to follow Christ. Yet he seemed to be sufficient or equal to any task, full of confidence and joy. He was "pressing toward the mark for the prize of the high calling of God in Christ Jesus." The goal or prize has its own inspiration. There is nothing quite like a great inspiration to motivate one to a great undertaking. But this was not the secret of Paul's strength. Recall his words: "In general and in particular, I have learned the secret of facing either poverty or plenty. I am ready for anything through the strength of the One who lives within me." This is the secret of his strength. He had found the supply of strength for all his needs in the glorious resources in Christ Jesus, his Lord. This can be the testimony of everyone who will turn, in faith, to the Lord Jesus Christ, for He is able to do exceeding abundantly above all that we may ask or think.

PRAYER

Father, we thank Thee that Thou hast
    a worthy goal for us to reach.
Enlighten our eyes that we may know
    what is the hope of this calling.
Grant that we may understand the exceeding
    greatness of Thy power,
To usward who believe. Amen.

X   A STANDING IN GRACE

> *For it is a good thing that the heart*
> *be established with grace.*
>
> — Hebrews 13:9

ON THE DAY THAT STEPHEN was executed because of his faith in Christ, a great persecution burst upon the Church in Jerusalem. Saul, who had given silent assent to the death of Stephen, harassed the Church bitterly. He went from house to house, dragging out both men and women and having them committed to prison.

Saul, still breathing murderous threats against the disciples of the Lord, went to the high priest and begged him for letters to the synagogues in Damascus, so that, if he should find there any followers of the way, whether men or women, he could bring them back to Jerusalem as prisoners.

But on his journey, as he neared Damascus, a light from heaven suddenly blazed around him and he fell to the ground. Then he heard a voice speaking to him, saying, "Saul, Saul, why are you persecuting me?"

"Who are you, Lord?" asked Saul.

"I am Jesus whom you are persecuting," was the reply. "But now stand up and go into the city and there you will be told what you must do."

Saul had fallen into the hands of the living God, whose

ways are not man's ways. He had discovered the awesome presence of the Holy Other. Perhaps it would be more correct to say that Saul was overtaken by God's grace. From beginning to end, the Biblical record is an account of man's having been overtaken and caught up in the gracious acts of God.

Years later, Saul, whom we now know as Paul, said, "But what I am now I am by the grace of God." Man's true identity and source of grace are in Jesus Christ.

God's gracious action on behalf of man is crucially important. Impossible of psychological analysis is the sudden and overpowering irruption of the life of God in a human soul. Two things have been accomplished — a new relationship and a new life. In this new relationship man experiences something which he has never had before — that is freedom. However varied its structure, the face of freedom is recognizable. It means more than larger grazing lands, elbow room, no fences, and no restrictions. It means exemption or release from slavery or imprisonment which was brought on by sin. It means exploring the regions of man's relations to God and man where freedom is not checkmated by wild fear.

This new relationship with God is life of a new quality into which one is begotten by God. One enters upon this new life with a new nature, a new self, in exchange for the old self which is given up. The new self is not a finished product when one receives it. As a young child, with proper care and direction, grows into maturity, so the new self, nurtured upon the things of God, develops into a life of beauty and of praise to God. On the other hand, rebellion and neglect stunt the new life and prevent its growth and development.

The present age is evil. Satanic powers still rule in the world. It lies in the arms of Satan. He is the father of those who, having had their minds blinded by him, belonging to what is below, loving it, perhaps rich in it, opposing Christ, are his children. They live blindfolded in the world of illusion and are cut off from the life of God through ignorance and insensitiveness. They have stifled their consciences and have surrendered themselves to sensuality, practicing any form of impurity which lust may suggest. The air is full of new and strange teachings that fascinate many by their very novelty. The new is not always wrong any more than the old is always right. The teachers of error are experts in their presentation of lies. In their cleverness and trickiness they practice deceit.

It is a mistake to assume that our fight against the spiritual agents from the very headquarters of evil is just in the field of religion as such. Even in a free society the powers that be are charged with the impulse to turn men into precise, predictable automata. Many men of power seem to have as their main purpose the elimination or neutralization of the independent individual, the independent voter, consumer, worker, owner, thinker — and every device they employ seems to aim at turning man into a manipulable, animated instrument, which is Aristotle's definition of a slave.

The never-ending task of finishing the new self, of transcending the limits of one's own physical being is in the power of God's grace. Grace, by its very nature, is much

more powerful in its working than evil. Hear God speak
through the Scripture:

> For it is a good thing
> that the heart be established
> with grace.
> — *Hebrews 13:9*

The words of this text are pertinent. In the atmosphere
of so many windy (like a hurricane or tornado) theories
only the heart which is fully established in an experience
with God's grace in Christ is stable. Grace may lead one
into a new relationship with God and here to take a stand
in happy certainty of the glorious future in store for him.
It is by the grace of God, the free, happy gift of His good
will toward men, the saving and preserving grace, that one
receives the spirit of a sound mind. It is also by this same
grace that one keeps the spirit of a sound mind. The new
man can now live a self-controlled, just and pious life, and
taste the sweetness of God's Word and the spiritual forces
of the age to come.

If the finding and saving of man is the first work of grace,
his emancipation from the fruitless moralism of the old sin-
ful nature is surely another accomplishment. This standing
in grace, then, is a matter of faith on man's part and generosity on God's part. Since it is by faith on man's part
and generosity on God's part, the security of His promise
of complete salvation is within reach of all men.

The gentle power of grace in its working is more powerful than that of evil. It is the most elusive factor in all one's
religious experience. It is like the tiny tendrils of a vine
which seem to have no strength in them, yet they find their

way into a crevice and split the hardest rock. The annals of history are full of stories which tell how grace can turn great sinners into saints, how grace takes one's limited life and releases it from its bondage into new and fresh experiences.

The working of grace may also be compared with the working of the great locks of Sault Ste. Marie, Michigan. The great freighter steams slowly to rest within the locks and seems to be trapped. But the hidden gateways are opened and the waters pour in and lift the vessel until finally it is on a level with the lake. Then the gates open and the ship steams forth upon the broad expanse of Lake Superior.

Life is so much like that. How often one needs to be lifted to higher levels of spiritual insight, courage, and power! The prophet Ezekiel, brooding and dejected at Chebar, suddenly saw the heavens open and said, "The Spirit lifted me up." It was upon this higher level that he saw a restored nation and a redeemed people. Three times Paul begged the Lord that his physical handicap be taken from him. The Lord's reply was, "My grace is enough for you; for where there is weakness, my power is shown the more completely." This is God's alternative answer. The burden remained but God's grace came in under to carry it.

Man's standing in grace may be corrupted or misunderstood. A common concept of freedom in America today is freedom from all restraint. Don't be under any illusions; one cannot follow the desires of the lower nature and stay free. A man's harvest in life will depend entirely on what he sows. If he sows for his own lower nature, his harvest will be slavery, decay and death.

Every failure to obey God's laws is sin, but there is no cause for despair. Sin that is not a deliberate embracing of evil can be overcome in the grace of God. Remember the words of John:

> But if a man should sin, remember that our advocate before the Father is Jesus Christ the righteous, the one who made personal atonement for our sins, (and for those of the rest of the world as well).
> — *I John* 2:1, 2 *(Phillips)*

Grace does not offer a cheap or an easy forgiveness that becomes merely a condoning of another person's sin. Neither is the sinner in any sense let off. But rather, forgiveness is placed on a moral foundation. Forgiveness is made possible because Jesus made atonement for our sins.

God's gracious forgiveness cannot be bought. It is a free gift. But there are certain conditions man must meet. In the first place, the measure of forgiveness received at God's hands is in direct ratio to the conscious need of forgiveness. Those who feel themselves overwhelmingly in debt and turn to God with a penitent cry are forgiven.

> For none, O Lord, has perfect rest
> For none is wholly free from sin;
> And they who fain would serve Thee best
> Are conscious most of wrong within.
> — *Henry Twells*

Secondly, divine forgiveness and human willingness to forgive are joined together. The message of Jesus in this regard is unequivocal:

> For if you forgive other people their failures,
> your Heavenly Father will also forgive you. But if
> you will not forgive other people, neither will your
> Heavenly Father forgive you your failures.
> — *Matthew 6:14, 15 (Phillips)*

This message is spoken too frequently and with too clear an emphasis to be denied. The proper attitude toward others is an ever-flowing spirit of forgiveness.

> O man, forgive thy mortal foe,
> Nor ever strike him blow for blow;
> For all the souls on earth that live
> To be forgiven must forgive.
> Forgive him seventy times and seven:
> For all the blessed souls in heaven
> Are both forgivers and forgiven.
> — *Tennyson*

Shakespeare wrote, "All the world's a stage . . . and one man in his time plays many parts." Some men are called upon to play a more difficult part than others. For instance, literary history relates no stranger story than Jeremiah's. In a very real sense it is the narrative of a poet's pilgrimage from the valley of dry bones to the Mount of Transfiguration. The years of his life were characterized by the baffling mental conflict of one who lives in extremes. Always there was the terrible tension of cross purposes, the agony of frantic self-analysis, the fear of ill-timed conclusions. Pity and pitilessness fought to master his emotions. It seemed as if he must forever waver between faith and doubt.

Jeremiah began his ministry in the thirteenth year of

Josiah's reign, about 627 B.C. His work extended until some time after the destruction of Jerusalem, at least until 586 B.C. The last glimpse we have of him is among the exiles in Egypt.

These years represent a tragic era for Jeremiah's people. Judah had lost all sense of virtue. Her sin was worse than that of any heathen nation. Religion had degenerated into the worship of idols. Jeremiah must preach a message of judgment which did not save, but rather hardened their hearts. He saw his people destroyed by the sword, carried away into captivity, and scattered to the winds.

Perhaps the most amazing fact concerning this impassioned man of Anathoth is that he could be so melancholy without becoming cynical. Not once did he lose confidence in the purpose of God or in the spiritual capacity of man. The grace of God gave him strength for the task that seemed overwhelming.

Later literature was to capture the same heroic spirit of men who found wisdom and strength in God's grace. In his "Summoner's Tale," Chaucer bitterly denounced the mercenary friar who gleaned his people's pocketbooks upon the pretense of praying for their souls and then served them mockeries and fables. Only two centuries after the ribald author of the Canterbury Tales had died, John Milton rebuked a corrupted English clergy in his "Lycidas." The world will never forget his simple, direct charge against them: "The hungry sheep look up, and are not fed." Nor is the present age without echo of the prophet's denunciation of ecclesiasticism. In a sonnet whose acidity is intensified by the restraint of its style, Edna St. Vincent Millay decried the spiritual apathy of the modern church as she wrote the lines of "To Jesus on His Birthday."

Perhaps the poet, John Greenleaf Whittier, has more perfectly voiced Jeremiah's lament than most:

> I ask no organ's soulless breath
> To drone the themes of life and death,
> No altar candle-lit day,
> No ornate wordman's rhetoric-play
> No cool philosophy to teach
> Its bland audacities of speech
> To double-tasked idolaters —
> Themselves their gods and worshippers.
> No pulpit hammered by the fist
> Of loud asserting dogmatist
> Who borrows for the Hand of love
> The smoking thunderbolts of Jove.
> I know how well fathers taught,
> That work the later school men wrought;
> I reverence old-time faith and men,
> But God is near us now as then;
> His force of love is still unspent;
> His hate of sin as imminent;
> And still the measure of our needs
> Outgrows the cramping bounds of creeds;
> The manna gathered yesterday
> Already savors of decay.

Here is love that truly takes upon itself the burden of a people's sin. One does not need to be a prophet, minister, or poet to play this part. But he will need a double portion of God's grace.

The late Samuel M. Shoemaker suggests several ways in which grace permeates the soul of man. Sometimes grace is given in a sharp stream to meet a crisis in life, to give control in sorrow, courage in danger, wisdom in making a decision. One may only know afterward that he has been helped. Sometimes grace is pervasive, atmospheric. Consider how a woman may take a dress out of a bag where it has gotten mussed, and there is not time to have it pressed before dinner. She turns on the hot water in the bathroom and hangs up the dress in the increasing moisture until some of the wrinkles come out. Grace is, in a sense, like steam, which, in its own pervasive way, can do the work of a hot iron. The cloth comes right because the tiny particles of moisture go all through it and take out the creases. In a like manner grace permeates the soul when the soul is as exposed to it as the garment is to the steam.

The question now arises — what is the channel through which one receives this all-embracing grace of God? First of all, it is through Jesus Christ that we have confidently entered into this new relationship of grace, and in him we take our stand in grace. He is our advocate before God. It is for His sake that God has shown any favor toward men. Let there be no self-delusion here; one's standing in grace is in Jesus Christ.

Secondly, God has chosen the Church for a channel of His grace. Note the vision of Ezekiel. He wrote about a river issuing from the threshold of the temple. It was a vision of the river of the grace of God — God's mercy, God's loving-kindness, His steadfast love — flowing in a mighty stream from the temple. It was a river that was full, deep, life-giving — because the water flowed from the sanctuary of God.

The work of the Church is one of making reality more enticing than fantasy. She makes a profession of drawing people into the arena of real fellowship with God and with the saints. Where there is real fellowship, there is real giving. For truly, to meet others in the fellowship of worship is to give and to receive something of what each one is as a person. The gift of giving oneself in worship and the response of God toward the giver establishes that communion which makes it possible for man to receive the blessings of grace. Then, in a very real sense, men and women, boys and girls, become channels that carry the water of life abroad in the land.

Thirdly, one must follow the leading of the Holy Spirit, for this is the age of the Spirit. He lives in our hearts. It is His work to help man in his present limitations. Do not assume that the Spirit will first take over and do all that needs to be done. Ask Him to help you, then follow His leadership. He will open unto you the blessings of God's marvelous grace.

All of the resources of God are available to man; His promises are unfailing. It is up to man to avail himself of all the wonderful blessings which God has for him. We could wish that every man make the decision expressed in these lines from the pen of Sidney Lanier:

> As the marsh-hen secretly builds on the watery
> sod,
> Behold, I will build me a nest on the greatness
> of God:

I will fly in the greatness of God as the marsh-
hen flies,
In the freedom that fills all the space 'twixt
the marsh and the skies;
By so many roots as the marsh-grass sends in
the sod,
I will heartily lay me a-hold on the greatness
of God.

— Sidney Lanier

Prayer

Father, we come boldly unto the throne
of Thy matchless grace.
Grant that we may obtain mercy, and find
grace to help in a time of need. Amen.

XI GOD'S FINISHING TOUCHES

> *Being confident of this very thing, that he*
> *which hath begun a good work in you will per-*
> *form it until the day of Jesus Christ.*
>
> — Philippians 1:6

REMBRANDT USED TO SAY that a picture is finished when
the painting has expressed the artist's intention. According to that dictum there must be a very few of us who
can say, "I have reached perfection. My life expresses God's
intention." The contrary is true. To be honest, most men
would confess to a sense of personal imperfection, and a
great number to personal failure.

When we look at the heavens — the moon and the stars,
the work of God's hands — we are conscious of our weakness and frailty. We are impressed with our littleness and
insignificance. This mood is frequently spoken of in the
Holy Scriptures in the following symbols: withering grass,
the fading flower, the vanishing vapor, the wind, a worm,
a shadow.

There is another picture of man revealed in the Bible.
It is one of exaltation — man created a little lower than the
angels and crowned with glory and honor. He is wonder-
fully and fearfully made, with illimitable possibilities. In
this mood man soars on wings of boundless aspiration; he

is inspired by matchless hopes; he dreams the dream of
all humanity.

In Psalm 90, the Hebrew poet gathers up the two haunt-
ing dreams of man — the dream of a perfect work and the
dream of a perfect life — and flings them up to heaven in
the final petition with which the Psalm ends:

> And let the beauty of the Lord our God
>   be upon us:
> and establish thou the work of our hands
>   upon us;
> yea, the work of our hands establish
>   thou it.

These lines express something that is deep and funda-
mental in the human heart — the desire for the perfect work
and the perfect life.

> Great it is to believe the dream
> When we stand in youth by the starry stream;
> But a greater thing is to fight life through
> And say at the end, "The dream was true."
> — *Edwin Markham*

The words of the text implicitly carry this double aspect
of life. Take another good look at what Paul said, "Of one
thing I am certain: the One who started the good work in
you will bring it to completion by the day of Jesus Christ."
This is a heartening message, full of inspiration and hope
for all who are distressed by the apparent futility of life.
The Infinite Artist will put the finishing touches upon man
and his work, but not without man's cooperation and part-

nership. In this work, we work with God, and that means that one is a field under God's cultivation.

One man in his lifetime may play many parts. It is true we cannot all be great artists, musicians, poets or philosophers, but we all have some talent or capacity which equips us with tools to work with. One man may break up the fallow ground and grub out the thorns. Another may come and plant the good seeds. Still another may come and water. History is full of Christian men and women who became pivotal people — such as Washington, Lincoln, Luther, Livingstone, and countless others. All workers in this world are exposed to conditions and circumstances which make for discouragement and despair. A striving, and a striving, and ending in nothing may seem to sum up the story of many a life. It is God that giveth the increase. He adds the finishing touches. His is the touch which saves from failure and defeat.

If a man longs to see his work perfected, much more he desires to see his life crowned with perfection. Like every competitor in athletic events, he goes into serious training, taking tremendous pains for the crown of life. He is no shadow boxer; he really fights! He longs to be perfectly whole.

Alongside this passion for perfection is the sense of our pathetic failure to achieve it. One finds himself not doing what he really wants to do but doing what he really loathes. He has the will to do good, but not the power.

The frustrated moral struggle is not final. The end is not yet. The One who has begun a good work in your life will not forsake it. One thing is sure: God is faithful to all His children. He will add the finishing touches — see that you do your part.

The frailty and brevity of human life may be offset by the supply from the glorious resources in Christ Jesus. Everyone must recognize that supply lines are essential and important in any line of warfare or defense. They are equally indispensable and important for the Christian, for we depend upon divine resources for renewal and power.

What are these supply lines? Let the writer name three. The first is prayer; the second is the Bible; the third is the Church.

Prayer, to Jesus, was as common as breathing and as essential as air. He began the day with prayer; here it is the girding of the loins for toil. In the evening time He prayed; here it is primarily prayer of disburdenment. He prayed at midday; here it is refreshment for mind and spirit. He prayed briefly before each meal; here it is acknowledgment of God as Creator and Provider. "Men ought always to pray and not to faint," He declared.

One day while Jesus was praying in a certain place, and after He had finished, it happened that one of His disciples said, "Lord, teach us how to pray, as John used to teach his disciples."

"When you pray," returned Jesus, "you should say, 'Father, may your name be honored — may your kingdom come! Give us each day the bread we need, and forgive us our sins, for we forgive anyone who owes anything to us; and keep us clear of temptation.' "

— *Luke 11:2-4 (Phillips)*

Jesus gave this prayer to the twelve disciples, not to be their only prayer, but to serve as a model or a pattern to show them what manner of prayer they should offer before the throne of God. According to David Smith, the model prayer has several striking characteristics. It is *brief* — recalling the Lord's warning against vain repetitions in the prayers of the heathen and the long prayers of the Pharisees. It is *simple* — suiting the lips of a little child. It is *catholic* — addressing our Heavenly Father. It is *spiritual* — concerning itself primarily with God's glory, His kingdom, and His will, and secondarily, with the simple needs of man.

Let us assume that we recognize the need for spiritual reinforcement, the question now arises: how does one get the most from the supply line of prayer? I hear people say, "I pray, but nothing happens." The rules of prayer are simple. One must pray in the only way a man can — in faith. The man who approaches God must have faith in two things. First, he must believe that God exists. Second, he must believe that it is worth a man's while to try to find God.

Let one approach the throne of grace with complete sincerity or honesty. Don't be under any illusions — you cannot make a fool of God! Prayer must be intelligent. Recall the words of Paul, "I am therefore determined to pray with my spirit and my mind." One shall, if he is wise, pray persistently; for prayer is not the mumbling over of stereotyped formulae, but a serious and strenuous business demanding the undivided energy of mind and heart. One shall pray humbly. He comes to God with that same exalted lowliness with which a loving and trusting child climbs into the lap of an understanding parent. One shall pray in the name of Jesus. To pray, using the phrase, "in Jesus name," as a magic wand, is not praying in the name of Jesus. To pray in the name of Jesus is to acknowledge that He is our only advocate before God. For He is the perfect High Priest, who intercedes on our behalf.

For the Christian the Bible is many things. It opens the mind to the full salvation which comes through believing in Jesus Christ. The Scriptures are the comprehensive equipment of the man of God, and they fit him fully for all branches of his work. The Word is both our defensive and our offensive weapon against Satan and all his forces. But I hear people say, "I read the Bible and get nothing from it."

A question which Jesus asked a certain lawyer may be appropriate here. How readest thou? There are two common attitudes toward the Bible. One is to regard the Bible as one does a favorite recording of music. He takes his favorite verses or selections, puts them on the record player and listens to them for comfort and satisfaction. I do not mean that one should not have favorite verses and selections, but there is a better and truer way for high fidelity and a living message from the Bible. The Bible is a live program with the all-wise and loving God on the other end.

God speaks to us personally through His Word. Perhaps one needs to read more prayerfully, thoughtfully, imaginatively, and widely. Then the voice of God will leap from the printed page and speak to his personal needs.

The perfecting of a life which has been marred and scarred by evil is a work of art. One may ask the question, "Can the Lord Jesus do anything for one who has many times broken the laws of health?" Before answering this question, let us look at the following story:

Dr. Austin S. Weiberger, Western Reserve University, Cleveland, reported recently in a talk before the American Cancer Society's science writers seminar that human red blood cells that are born to be bad can be straightened out— like some wayward juvenile delinquent by the right influences.

By the same token, scientists have been able to make normal young blood cells go bad by putting them into intimate contact with the wrong influences. For instance, Dr. Weisberger took certain genetic proteins from blood producing bone marrow of persons ill with sickle cell anemia — a type of anemia that tends to strike Negroes and dark-skinned persons, apparently from an inherited susceptibility. By incubating the sickle cell protein material with normal but young red blood cells, he found that the normal blood cells come out of the brew with certain abnormal traits — resembling the traits of the sickle cells.

He also did the reverse of the experiment, taking blood-producing marrow from normal individuals, extracting the genetic protein from it, and incubating this protein with young sickle cells. The sickle cells came out of this experiment with traits of normal red blood cells. These experiments indicate that the genetic protein material from cells can somehow alter the genetic or inherited traits of other cells.

The preceding account of a medical discovery is an example of the marvelous things man can do. How much more marvelous is the finishing work of Christ in the life of man! The greatest experiment of all time has proved that the Infinite Artist can and does perfect the one He created. He has chosen the Church, or churches, of Jesus Christ for this wonderful work.

How marvelous, how audacious is the Apostle Paul's language when he sets forth the ineffable mystery of the Lord's churches. "We are members of his body." "Your bodies are members of Christ." "We that are many, are one body in Christ, and severally members one of another." "As the body is one and hath many members, and all the members of the body, being many, are one body, so also is Christ . . . and whether one member suffer, all the members suffer with it; or a member be glorified, all the members rejoice with it."

"Ye are no more strangers and sojourners," wrote Paul to the Ephesians, "but ye are fellow-citizens with the saints, and of the household of God . . . Christ Jesus himself being the chief corner stone; in whom each several building, fitly framed together, groweth into a holy temple in the Lord; in whom ye also are builded together for a habitation of God in the Spirit" (2:19-22, asv). This is one of the master-thoughts of apostolic days.

The Infinite Artist has chosen the Church as an agent through whom He will accomplish the finishing touches to the lives of men. This is a work of art. But the Church of Jesus Christ is well able to do it. For He has placed within her hands His divine resources whereby the frailty and brevity of human life may be offset. Also, He has given gifted men, empowered by His Spirit, to properly equip and nourish the new life until it arrives at real maturity —

that measure of development which is meant by "the full-ness of Christ."

It is not unusual to hear people say, "I go to church, but it doesn't mean anything to me." Perhaps these come to church to be entertained, or for some other ulterior motive. Some come to church, who, for one reason or other, are in no spiritual or physical condition to worship. Their hearts are not prepared for worship, neither are they prepared to receive what God has for them. It is no wonder that they fail to find real fellowship with the saints of God and to hear God speak to their hearts. It is the humble, open, receptive, contrite, surrendered spirit that counts with God.

In this volume, the writer has sought to trace the beneficial design, the graciousness of the divine intention, in the painful discipline of life. It is hoped that, in some measure, the reader's capacity for responsibility has been stimulated, thereby helping him to become aware of the full spectrum of possibilities for personal meaning and values of life.

If there are things one cannot fully understand, dealings that seem unduly severe, providences that perplex, trials that threaten to overwhelm, experiences that shadow one's life, let him bear them in faith. The Captain of our salvation was made perfect by suffering.

PRAYER

Our Father, who desireth health and wholeness
    and holiness in Thy children,
We come to receive Thy grace.
Forgive us the many times that we have broken
    Thy laws of health.

Correct our errors made in ignorance.
Restore our hearts to wholeness and tenderness.
Help us to bring healing and wholeness to our
    fellows.
This we ask in Jesus' name. Amen.

The Spirit of a Sound Mind does not attempt to provide pat answers to problems, nor does it propose comfortable conclusions. Rather, this book offers positive insights into God's pattern for effective living — prepared by an experienced minister and counselor.

Dr. Cobb's answer to the dilemma facing mankind is based not only on soundly Biblical principles, it is also founded upon thoroughly workable and practical psychological precepts. He asserts that even as man's troubles begin with rebellion against God, the solution to his problem lies in commitment and conformity to God's plan for man.

Dr. John Ross Cobb, native of Greenville, South Carolina, is a 1945 graduate of Mississippi College, Clinton, Mississippi, with a Bachelor of Arts degree, majoring in history. He is also a graduate of New Orleans Baptist Theological Seminary, New Orleans, Louisiana, with Bachelor of Divinity, Master of Theology, and Doctor of Theology degrees, majoring in New Testament Greek and fellow in that department for four years.

He has pastored Baptist churches in Alabama and Mississippi for the past eighteen years, having served the Raymond Baptist Church, Raymond, Mississippi, for five years, and now, for more than nine years has served as pastor of First Baptist Church, Inverness, Mississippi.